D1071421

Life Is Beautiful, but Not for Jews

FILMMAKERS SERIES
edited by
ANTHONY SLIDE

Life Is Beautiful, but Not for Jews

Another View of the Film by Benigni

Kobi Niv

*Translated from the Hebrew
by Jonathan Beyrak Lev*

Filmmakers Series, No. 107

The Scarecrow Press, Inc.
Lanham, Maryland, and Oxford
2003

SCARECROW PRESS, INC.

Published in the United States of America
by Scarecrow Press, Inc.
A wholly owned subsidiary of
The Rowman & Littlefield Publishing Group, Inc.
4501 Forbes Boulevard, Suite 200, Lanham, Maryland 20706
www.scarecrowpress.com

PO Box 317
Oxford
OX2 9RU, UK

I wish to express my gratitude to the Hubert Burda Center for Innovative
Communications at Ben Gurion University of the Negev in Israel for its support for the translation of the book into English.

British Library Cataloguing in Publication Information Available

Library of Congress Cataloging-in-Publication Data

Niv, Kobi.
  [Hachaim yafim aval lo li-Yehudim. English]
  Life is beautiful, but not for Jews : another view of the film by
Benigni / Kobi Niv. — 1st ed.
      p. cm. — (Filmmakers series ; no. 107)
    ISBN 0-8108-4875-9 (alk. paper)
    1. Vita è bella (Motion picture)   2. Holocaust, Jewish (1939–1945),
in motion pictures. I. Title. II. Series.
PN1997 .V5373 N5813 2003
791 .43'72—dc21

                                                         2003010781

Contents

Acknowledgments

I would like to express my profound gratitude to all the people who helped me in the complex process of writing this book:

To my friends, Savi Gabizon, Adi Gold, Hanoch Marmari, Meir Schnitzer, and Professor Dov Shinar, who read early versions, commented wisely and lovingly, and helped give the manuscript shape and direction.

To the experts and colleagues who contributed illuminating explanations and references—Rafi Adar, Alon Altaras, Dr. Yishay Almog, Zvi Yanay, and Professor Nurith Kenaan-Kedar.

To my father, Moshe, who supported and helped me, and to my son, Uri, who gave me insight.

To Gabbi Padovano, who translated from Italian anything I needed and who helped me—with real dedication and out of identification with the book's argument—far beyond the requirements of the job of a translator; without her, the book would be truly incomplete.

To Itamar Orian, né Jerzy (Jurek) Trybel, for the permission to quote a segment from his videotaped testimony.

To my Hebrew publishers, Nathan Beyrak and Eleonora Lev, for their hospitality in every meaning of the word.

A special thank you to Nathan Beyrak for the Joker.

Many thanks to the book's Hebrew editor, Eleonora Lev, who, with much love, dedication, and great skill, did a wonderful job.

And most of all, thanks to Einat, my wife.

In the name and memory of all members of the Weinberger and Schwarzman families murdered in the Holocaust—

My grandfather, Jacob, after whom I am named,

My grandmother, Rachel, after whom my sister is named,

My aunt, my mother's sister, Esther,

My aunt, my father's sister, Ida,

My aunt, my father's sister, Itka Stein, née Weinberger, and her one-year-old son, whose name we do not know to this day and who was shot to death together with Itka when she refused to part with him.

Before I Begin

SOMETHING HERE'S A LITTLE TOO CUTE

Before I saw *Life Is Beautiful*,[1] I loved it very much.

The basic concept of the film, as I had read and heard about it, seemed to me absolutely brilliant—a Jewish father successfully passing his small son through the hellfire of the Holocaust while convincing the child that it's all just a game of adventure, thus saving the boy's life.

Two wonderful scenes from the film, repeatedly shown on television, increased my eagerness to see the film and my expectation to like it very much when I did—the one in which the father explains to his son why a sign posted in a shop window in their hometown forbids the entry of dogs and Jews, and the one in which the father "translates" for the child from German into Italian the menacing commands barked by the concentration camp guard, turning them in the process into the "rules" of the imaginary "game."

When, on top of this, I observed the chorus of enthusiastic praise from critics and commentators; the numerous awards bestowed in countries around the world on Roberto Benigni, the film's screenwriter, director, and star, long before he won his eventual Oscars; and the excited reactions of friends and acquaintances who had seen the film—I became positively prejudiced in favor of *Life Is Beautiful* and its fervent fan before ever actually seeing it.

But then I went to see the film, and it spoiled everything.

As the first hour of the film dragged on, I was silently growing more and more irritated. I had been promised a film about a father and his son winningly making their way through the Holocaust, and what I got instead was, to my taste, just another mediocre, annoyingly banal comedy. Its compulsive attempts to force some laughs out of the audience bordered on the embarrassing.

After the long hour of banality, the Holocaust finally arrived. At first, this part of the film, which included those two truly remarkable scenes that I was already familiar with from repeated showings on television, seemed to me not only promising but also made it seem that the film would indeed fulfill its promise. Yet at the same time, I felt a growing anxiety, a sense that something was wrong.

The concentration camp to which the father and son were taken was just too good, too nice, too amusing a place, too devoid of death. It even seemed, in a way, not much worse than my basic training camp in the army—a sort of not-too-tough labor camp.

And then came the scene in which a Jewish prisoner is wounded in the arm during forced labor, and a German guard immediately sends him—as if it were the most self-evident everyday routine—to the infirmary. The prisoner later returns to the barrack and tells the film's main character, Guido (played by Roberto Benigni), that his arm has been stitched in twenty different points. Guido's son, Giosue (for reasons I'll make clear later on, I reject "Joshua" as a translation of the child's name and stay throughout with the Italian original), who believes—because that is what his father told him in an earlier scene—that everything that happens in the camp is part of a game played for points, responds to this by proudly whispering to his father: "We got more!"[2]

This is it, I told myself; that does it.

Any film, whatever its genre, that suggests that this was how life in a concentration camp during the Holocaust looked like; any film that implies, however unwittingly, that the modus operandi of this particular camp—quite tough but still tolerable, and almost humane and decent, compared to the genuine article—was somehow the norm; a film that portrays a sick or wounded Jewish prisoner rushed to the infirmary to be stitched and tended to and then returned, healed or bandaged, to his barrack—is more than a display of misunderstanding, to use a neutral word, of the basic facts of life, and of death, in a World War II German concentration camp. It amounts in fact to a distorted presentation of the Holocaust as a whole.

Suddenly I saw it: the film was a total falsification. And what made it a falsification was not what was shown on the screen, but precisely what was absent from it.

It is not that there were no infirmaries, of a sort, in the concentration camps, or that the camps' prisoners were never treated in them (most often by doctors and medics who were prisoners themselves) before being returned to the barracks and to forced labor.

But this, like so many other routine features of everyday life in the camps, was a deliberate, sinister grotesque, in the spirit of the slogan "Arbeit Macht Frei"—"Work Makes You Free." Life in the camps was a methodical, monstrous parody of order and reason. Coinciding with a system of heinous abuse, designed to break the prisoners' spirit each day anew and to hold them in a constant state of terror and degradation, was a mock display of "normal procedures" that was strictly adhered to—of a regular, rational administration taking the necessary and expectable care of the needs of the hundreds of thousands of people herded into these places. This included supplying some rudimentary sleeping and feeding arrangements, some deception of healthcare and hygiene, and even rules and "laws" complete with a "judicial system."

And it is exactly this sham "normality" that *Life Is Beautiful* chooses to present us with, while avoiding mention of nearly all of the rest. When we are shown a wounded prisoner who gets treated, but we do not get to see anything else—the brutality, the starvation, the beatings, the humiliation, the endless standing to attention day and night, or the daily executions—we are actually shown a softened, sugar-coated, and outright false version of the truth: a concentration camp lite.

There were, of course, instances of sick or wounded prisoners receiving medical care, sometimes even thoroughly adequate care. But the fact that a prisoner was, by luck, appropriately treated on any given day never meant that the very next day, the same prisoner would not be shot to death, thrown into the gas chamber, or murdered in some other fashion.

The best treatment, relatively speaking, was accorded to the Jews imprisoned in the Theresienstadt ghetto, an "exemplary" concentration camp in Czechoslovakia. The Germans used it precisely for this purpose: to mask the true nature of their "Final Solution." *Theresienstadt: Ein Dokumentarfilm aus dem judischen Siedlungsgebiet (Theresienstadt: A Documentary Film from the Self-governing Jewish Zone)*,[3] a famous German propaganda film, described the so-called peaceful life of the inhabitants of Theresienstadt, who were shown sitting in cafés, playing soccer, and so on. Representatives of the Red Cross were invited to see for themselves that life in the German ghettos and concentration camps was perfectly "normal," and that, contrary to the claims of the "Jewish propaganda machine," the inmates of these places were not really mistreated, let alone mass murdered. What these neutral visitors were not informed of was the fact that most of the inhabitants of Theresienstadt, including those whom they met on their visit as well as those who were forced to participate as "actors" and crew in the shooting of the propaganda film, were soon afterwards sent to the Auschwitz death camp, where nearly all of them were murdered by gas.

Thus, anyone even vaguely familiar with the historical truth must know that at one and the same time and side by side with this "normal" existence, the real routine of the camps went on. A sick or incapacitated prisoner who lost his ability to work could sometimes be taken to the surgery, bandaged, cured, and so forth. Or he could—more often than not, and without a moment's thought on the part of the camp guards—be shot to death on the spot, much the same way a broken-legged horse is or, worse still, the same way a cockroach is casually crushed underfoot.

Moreover, this representation of the Jews—or, rather, people classified as "Jews" according to the pseudoscientific "race theory"—as equivalent to insects or rodents served as both legal and psychological justification for other people, namely, European Christians—or at least those among them lucky enough to be classified as "Aryans"—to take active part in, or to passively assent to, the sustained, organized massacre of those designated as "Jews" at those times.

This was the deep, crucial core of the Holocaust phenomenon—the dehumanization of the Jews (and ultimately, by various degrees, of all other "racial enemies," including the physically and mentally handicapped, Gypsies, left-wingers, homosexuals, and others) and their arbitrary exclusion, by force of administrative directives, from the human race. What made the whole atrocity possible was the categorization of certain human beings as a strain of pests, essentially no different from rats or roaches—disgusting, filthy, parasitic creatures that spread deadly plagues (as the Jews were memorably depicted in the well-known Nazi propaganda film *Der ewige Jude* [*The Eternal Jew*]).[4] Simple considerations of hygiene, if nothing else, demanded their thorough elimination.

How strange, then, to encounter in *Life Is Beautiful* a "German concentration camp" resembling the fake "exemplary" one built by the Nazis themselves. No doubt, I thought to myself while watching the film, that your common Holocaust denier would very much welcome this type of portrayal of a "concentration camp."

From this point on, I was no longer able to view the film from any other perspective. As it drew closer to its ending, my discomfort steadily grew, and with it the realization that this film belittles and sanitizes the truth of the Holocaust, perhaps to the extent of outright denial.

And when, at the very end of the film, the predictable angel of salvation appeared riding a tank and turned out to be none other than a kitschy American soldier, I felt that I finally understood the entire story and purpose of this film. Someone's really got an eye out for an Oscar, I thought. And not only that—he's going to win it.

But that, of course, isn't the issue. The problem is that in a few years, or even today, when someone attempts to explain the historical truth about the fate of the Jews in German-occupied Europe, those whose only knowledge of the Holocaust is based on this film may counter, and not even out of malice, just in all innocence: "What are you talking about? What's that about someone killing the Jews? No way they killed any Jews. Yes, they made them work pretty hard, but that's about it. Far from that, actually—they were treated quite decently. Take *Life Is Beautiful*, which won an Oscar in Jewish-owned Hollywood. And don't you forget that this movie was very successful in Israel, too, and they wrote a lot of wonderful things about it. It shows they were not treated that horribly in the camps. For example, when they were wounded, they'd take them down to the infirmary, stitch their wounds. So what are you babbling about mass extermination?"

I saw the film with my wife, Einat. During the show, as usual when we go to the cinema, we did not exchange a word. But this time, we remained seated, silently, even after the film had ended. We waited until everyone left the theater, and only then, still silent, we left as well. We exchanged glances, but neither of us said a word until we reached the parking lot. Getting into the car, I said: "It is a little like denying the Holocaust, this film, isn't it?"

She responded by breaking into bitter tears.

"What's wrong?" I asked. "Why are you crying?"

Between sobs, she managed a choked reply: "It's Grandma."

Her grandmother died a few weeks earlier. *Life Is Beautiful* was the first film we went to see after the customary thirty days of mourning were over. Einat's grandmother, Yolana Berger, née Fux, was a survivor of the Auschwitz concentration camp. And without her uttering another word, I knew precisely why Einat was crying. She was crying out of a deep, searing sense of insult. She was crying because she felt that this film, *Life Is Beautiful,* mocked her grandmother, her life, her death, and her memory. It turned her grandmother's life, her struggles, her survival, the family she managed to raise after miraculously escaping death, her daughter, her granddaughter, the entire Holocaust, and the millions murdered in it, indeed it turned all of us—specifically Jews, but indeed human beings in general—into a cheap joke in pursuit of an Oscar.

Since then, I've seen the film many times and have read its script several dozen times—in the original Italian (with the help of a translator) and in its English and Hebrew translations. The conclusions that I've reached, brought forward in this work, are even harsher than our first spontaneous reactions and have much graver general implications.

Let me stress here that, not being an expert on the Holocaust, I did not set about analyzing the film as a historian. Instead, my point of departure was my own professional involvement with the cinema—as a scriptwriter and teacher of scriptwriting, and as an author of two books, one on the art and technique of screenwriting and the other on deciphering and interpreting the inherent meanings in scripts and in actual films.

My method of examination is nothing unusual—it is mainstream contemporary critique of artistic texts (visual, verbal, or other). It involves going under the surface and exploring the subtext, that is to say, the implied, silent assumptions and content behind the visible text and, ultimately, revealing the hidden—and, I believe, true—message of the film.

Needless to say, the outrage and anguish that *Life Is Beautiful* invoked in me, and my very interest in this movie, aren't purely professional. They doubtlessly originate in my personal connection with the subject matter—the persecution, torture, and mass murder of the Jews during the Second World War are a part of my past and present, of my heart and soul.

Many members of my family were murdered in the Holocaust, yet I would like to think that I am far from being obsessed with it in my everyday life. Neither am I one of those purists who would only allow a single, narrowly documentary approach to the question of depicting the Holocaust and its events, namely strictly documentary description. For many of these people, any other manner of addressing this unique historical event—for instance, through any kind of dramatization, let alone a comedy—is nothing short of heresy.

Quite the contrary. I believe, for example, that Art Spiegelman's *Maus*,[5] a comic-strip novel portraying the atrocities of the Holocaust as experienced by Spiegelman's father, in which the Germans are represented as cats and the Jews as mice, is one of the most wonderful and moving works created out of the Holocaust experience and its memory.

I myself wrote a script for a short film based on a story by a Holocaust survivor, Gavriel (Patia) Dagan, to which I gave the provocative title *Shoa Tova* (*Nice Little Holocaust*).[6] The film, produced in the early 1990s, ends with a child adopting a wounded dog run over and brought to her kibbutz by the Holocaust survivor, who arrives there to give a lecture on the annual Holocaust Commemoration Day. The girl names the dog "Shoa"—"Holocaust"—and, petting her, repeatedly says: "Shoa Tova, Shoa Tova"—"Nice little Holocaust, nice little Holocaust"—from which I took the title for the film. Giving a dog the name "Holocaust," and the revolting, unthinkable oxymoron "nice Holocaust," caused at the time great scandal in Israel, and there were some enraged demonstrations and calls to cancel the film's screening. But those who did see the film and realized its true intent knew that it was an honest appeal to hold and to caress, to soothe, to conciliate with, and to accept, individually as well as nationally, both the wounds of the Holocaust and its wounded.

The concept of Benigni's film—a Jewish father shielding his son from the true meaning of the Holocaust while they are both imprisoned in a concentration camp by letting the child see only a small part, just one specific, amusing "frame" of the big, horrifying picture, and creating for the child the illusion that this nice little "frame" he sees is in truth the entire event they are experiencing—seems not only legitimate to me but also remains, to my mind, a truly brilliant concept, just as it was before I saw the film.

What is problematic is the way this concept is realized in this particular film. In *Life Is Beautiful,* writer-director Benigni does to his audience exactly what the father played by the actor Benigni does to his screen son: he shows the audience just a small part, a very particular, doctored, cute little "frame" out of the whole picture. At the same time, he withholds from the viewers the full horrid picture, and he thus creates, or at least does not mind creating, in them the impression that this fake reality as described in the film is in fact what took place in the death camps and, by implication, what happened to the Jews in the Holocaust.

This is why we cried, my wife and I, and from that weeping my book begins.

THE MAGIC OF MANIPULATION

We go to the cinema to be excited. This simple, elementary truth is worth repeating, because, in my experience, even intelligent, sophisticated viewers tend to forget it from time to time. The power of the cinematic medium is so great and overwhelming, so hypnotizing, that it is sometimes difficult for us to discern the calculated mechanism of excitement that powers it.

Sitting in a darkened theater, we experience with others, mostly strangers, a sweeping, stirring, and potent emotional journey.

We sit in chairs arranged in rows, facing, as it were, the road ahead, as if in a futuristic spaceship or a fantastic time machine; and when the lights go out, we really do take off and are flown to another world. Until the lights come up again at the end of the film, we fully live, to the depths of our thoughts and emotions, in a fabricated world, transcending actual reality and obliterating it from our minds.

Thus, our experience of the cinema is that of a journey through an altered state of consciousness, a very real emotional journey in a completely artificial world.

Our "vehicle" for this journey is our sympathy with the film's protagonists. Our emotional journey is in fact theirs. Through this sympathy, we share their journey and endure their struggles and hardships all the way to the end, be it good or bad, happy or heartbreaking. When the journey ends, the film is over. The protagonists who won our sympathy have either won or lost. Their journey was either a success or a failure. The theater lights go up, and we wipe our tears of joy or sorrow, returning to reality from our emotional journey through the film's fictional world.

But is our emotional journey as viewers a spontaneous one, occurring in and of itself, incidentally, as the plot twists and turns? Of course it is not. For this journey, or film, is a "fiction"—that is to say, an invention. Someone invented and contrived it, deliberately concocted it. Whoever created the protagonists' journey, down to the last detail, created our emotional journey as well.

And this, again, is an elementary truth worth repeating: the film's creators, those who wrote, directed, and shot it, were the ones who sent the protagonists on their journey, put obstacles in their way and subjected them to dangers, and decided whether and how they would overcome these obstacles and escape those dangers, whether they would win or lose, and whether they would find love at the end of the journey or not.

Hence, it is the film's creators who create the viewer's emotional journey. They manipulate the viewers and program their emotional responses in front of the screen. Every frame, every move, every sound in each and every film is directed toward affecting the viewers' emotions at exactly the right moment. For the duration of the entire film, the creators lead the viewers according to the needs of the cinematic journey, from anxiety to relief, from relief to fear, from fear to terror to laughter, from laughter to sorrow to happiness, from happiness to tension to amazement, from amazement to glee to sadness, and so on.

The biography of the director Alfred Hitchcock by Donald Spoto[7] contains a true story as told by screenwriter Ernest Lehman. During the filming of their joint film *North by Northwest*,[8] Hitchcock took Lehman out to dinner.

He'd had a few Martinis, and in a rare moment of emotional intimacy, he put his hand on mine and whispered: "Ernie, do you realize what we're doing in this picture? The audience is like a giant organ that you and I are playing. At one moment, we play *this* note on them to get *this* reaction, and then we play *that* chord and they react *that* way. And someday we won't even have to make a movie—there'll be electrodes implanted in their brains, and we'll just press different buttons and they'll go 'ooooh' and 'aaaah' and we'll frighten them, and make them laugh. Won't that be wonderful?"

Hitchcock, as is evident from this story, not only knew his job well as a director but also understood what was behind it: a film, like any other work of art or entertainment—apart from anything else that can be said for or against it, and apart from any other kind of magic that can be attributed to it—is always an exercise in emotional manipulation. The emotional journey that the viewers experience while seeing the film is the result of this deliberate, more or less sophisticated manipulation that is played on them by the creators of the film, first and foremost by the director and the scriptwriter—with the help, of course, of the camera operators, the actors, the composer, and the rest of the crew who contributed to the finished product.

And yet the fact that each and every film is always a mechanism of manipulation does not mean that it is some sort of malicious conspiracy against the viewer, even if the drunk Hitchcock's electrode organ dream might be so construed.

There is, of course, any number of producers, scriptwriters, and directors on Hollywood's assembly lines who know their function well and heed the demands of their bosses; that is, they put the demands of the studio's accountants and stockholders before and above all other considerations. They proficiently design their films' emotional manipulation mechanism in a premeditated, even cynical way, expressly choosing the lowest-denominator target audience so as to achieve the greatest profit possible, based on opinion polls, focus groups, and all the other tricks of the marketing trade. But I am still willing to assume that the great majority of filmmakers, like the great majority of artists and entertainers in general, acts in good faith, creating their films' (or that of their works in other media) emotional manipulation not as a cheap trick in order to improve their financial status but out of an honest desire to tell a story, to say something meaningful about life and about the world, out of their natural talent and of what really interests them. In the end, I believe that most works of art and entertainment come out from deep within their creators' subconscious.

The difference between our definition of a "good" film and that of a "bad" one lies in whether or not the emotional manipulation—conscious or not—that a given film's creators tried to play on us indeed affected and moved us. This difference is personal and subjective, and so varies necessarily from one person to the next. If the manipulation worked, then the film truly stirred us, and we define it as a "good" one. If, for one reason or another, the film did not succeed in manipulating our emotions, did not excite us, left us indifferent and unsympathetic, or even annoyed and disgusted us, we define it as a "bad" one. There is nothing more to it.

The process, as I said, is purely subjective. There are films (or books, or musical pieces, or other works) that cause some people pleasure and move them to tears, whereas others can only remark, "How can anyone enjoy that boring garbage?" Examples abound, of course, in all artistic fields. But could we be excited, as it were, for the wrong reasons? Could it be that our feelings and gut reactions, upon which we usually rely as trustworthy guides to life, to everything happening around us, would deceive us?

The instant response to this question would be: "Absolutely not. When I cry, I cry. When I laugh, I laugh, and if I'm excited, I'm excited, and that's all the 'rightness' I need to know that I'm looking at an excellent piece of art."

The only problem is that we all have long lists of films, books, and so on, and of directors, writers, and so on, who not only leave us ice cold emotionally and utterly bored intellectually, but we just cannot understand how they are taken seriously by anyone. How can people be deceived by the cheap, hopelessly transparent manipulations—in our eyes, at least—of these terrible works and their creators?

And since it's all a matter of taste, others in turn may very well feel the same about the movies, books, and so on that we cherish and admire.

Which is to say: falling prey to emotional manipulation is something that happens to us all, all the time. Being mislead by emotions that someone else has deliberately instilled in us is a real risk for anyone. You don't have to be especially slow-witted or gullible, just human.

And this tendency is there, obviously, not only when we relate to art and entertainment but also in our relationship to other people. Most of us have had at least one relationship in which, looking back, sometimes years later, we see that we had been woefully mislead by our feelings. From the vantage point of the present, it is starkly clear that we gave our love to someone who was, unfortunately, unworthy of it. But when we are deeply in love, in the midst of emotional turmoil, nothing in the world can convince us we're wrong.

Most of us may remember how we once tried to convince a friend, say, that her partner doesn't suit her or is bad for her. But have we ever met anyone who had accomplished the feat of moving the suffering friend to stop her relationship with her inadequate or abusive partner? Usually the result is the opposite: the unhappy friend cuts off all ties with the concerned third party.

Trying to convince a person in love that he or she is wrong is in all probability a mission impossible. I realize that this is the mission I took upon myself in writing this book.

The film *Life Is Beautiful* was screened all over the world and met everywhere with huge success. The tens of millions who flocked to see it made it the most profitable Italian film ever (at the time this was written, it grossed close to a quarter of a billion dollars). It was also showered with endless praise and almost unanimous acclaim in the media wherever it played and won almost every possible cinematic award. Dissenting voices were few and far between.

This enormous success proves that the vast majority of the film's viewers enjoyed a positive emotional experience: they felt sympathy, sorrow, joy, and excitement. They fell in love with this film and embraced it as a beautiful, cleansing, and maybe even transcendent experience—as a moving and inspiring story of love and redemption.

None of this happened to me; my experience of this film was entirely, and distressingly, different. In this book I attempt to explain why, in my opinion, *Life Is Beautiful* is very far from being the innocent, joyful, and enchanting film it pretends to be.

NOTES

1. *La vita é bella*, script: Roberto Benigni and Vincenzo Cerami, director: Roberto Benigni, Italy 1998.

2. All quotes from the film and script were taken from the Hebrew subtitles and the following sources: Roberto Benigni and Vincenzo Cerami, *La vita é bella* (Turin, Italy: Einaudi, 1998); Roberto Benigni and Vincenzo Ce-

rami, *Life Is Beautiful,* trans. Lisa Taroccio (London: Faber and Faber, 1999); and Roberto Benigni and Vincenzo Cerami, *Hachaim Yafim,* trans. Lea Stagman (Hod-Hasharon, Israel: Astrolog Publishing, 1999).

3. *Theresienstadt: Ein Dokumentarfilm aus dem judischen Siedlungsgebiet,* known also as *Der Führer schenkt den Juden eine Stadt* or *Wie schön ist Theresienstadt (The Führer Donates a Town to the Jews* or *How Beautiful Is Theresienstadt),* director: Kurt Gron, Germany 1944–1945. Gron, a Jew, worked under the orders and close supervision of the S.S., and shortly after the filming ended he was deported to Auschwitz, where he was murdered.

4. *Der ewige Jude,* script: Eberhard Taubert, director: Fritz Hippler, Germany 1940.

5. Art Spiegelman, *Maus: A Survivor's Tale* (New York: Random House, 1986).

6. *Shoa Tova (Nice Little Holocaust),* script: Kobi Niv, director: Orna Ben-Dor, Israel 1992.

7. Donald Spoto, *The Dark Side of Geniusaaaaa:The Life of Alfred Hitchcock* (New York: Da Capo Press, 1999).

8. *North by Northwest,* script: Ernest Lehman, director: Alfred Hitchcock, United States 1959.

Chapter 1

Hitler's Holiday Camp

Any attempt to duplicate or reconstruct a Nazi concentration camp in a film is inherently problematic. It is, of course, possible to reconstruct, relatively easily and quite accurately, the less important aspects, namely the camp's physical features—the shape and size of the barracks and bunk beds, the number of people, the different marks of identification on the prisoners' uniforms, the German jailers' insignia, and various other technicalities. But a true-to-life recreation of the most important feature—the actual living conditions, if "living" is indeed the appropriate word here, of the people who were imprisoned in those places—is all but impossible.

We are talking about hundreds of thousands of people driven one day out of their homes, dispossessed of all their property, and sometimes brutally separated from their loved ones, whom they would often see starving to death or murdered right in front of their eyes. Some were first isolated in ghettos, in inhuman conditions, for many months or even years before being transported by train to an unknown destination, together with a mass of people as scared as they were, crowded like so much cattle into cattle cars, with no food, water, or lavatories. En route, which usually took several long days and nights, the weak were often trampled or died of thirst or suffocation. The rest reached, at the journey's end, an unknown destination somewhere at the edge of the continent, where, as they found out immediately upon arrival, the reign of terror was even fiercer. After going through a "selection" process, they were ordered to hand over their clothes. Those who were not immediately exterminated were made to wear tattered

1

prisoners' uniforms. They were forcibly shaved (which did not prevent the lice that plagued the camps to swarm them, too, almost immediately), starved, beaten, systematically degraded, and driven to hard labor for many hours per day, in all weather conditions—extreme heat or cold—without adequate nutrition or any real rest.

And so, the vast majority of those who were not arbitrarily, methodically massacred immediately upon arrival to the camp but were taken in as regular, registered inmates did not survive for long either. In a matter of weeks or months, almost all died of starvation, disease, and exhaustion, or they were killed by gunshot or by gas when they took ill or when their capacity for work had been finally depleted.

All this was described by the Jewish Italian writer Primo Levi, an Auschwitz survivor whose works stand among the most important and impressive of the thousands of personal testimonies we have of daily life in the "concentration camp universe." Roberto Benigni said in press interviews that he had read Levi's works and that he admired and cherished them.

In his book *The Drowned and the Saved*, Primo Levi wrote:

> Even apart from the hard labor, the beatings, the cold, and the illnesses, the food ration was decisively insufficient for even the most frugal prisoner; the physiological reserves of the organism were consumed in two or three months, and death by hunger, or by diseases induced by hunger, was the prisoner's normal destiny, avoidable only with additional food. Obtaining that extra nourishment required a privilege—large or small, granted or conquered, astute or violent, licit or illicit—whatever it took to lift oneself above the norm.[1]

Those very few who did manage to rise above the common prisoner's norm, that is to say, to somehow obtain a "privilege" that enabled them to get the essential added nutrition Primo Levi writes about, endured in that ocean of death. And we must remember that all of this—the starvation, the humiliation, the torture, the lice, the constant mortal fear—went on and on, for months and years, without any of the prisoners (in contrast with the inmates of "normal" contemporary prisons—and this difference is crucial, as far as the imprisoned person is concerned) having any idea as to when, if ever, liberation would come, and with it, maybe, an end to the suffering.

So even if we consider these prisoners physically, from the out-side, we are generally talking about broken people, all skin and bone, eyes sunken in terminal degradation and total despair—specters of human beings, literally the walking dead.

How is it possible then to approximate even the physical appear-ance of the people in the recreated concentration camp? Do you ask the actors to go on a brutal diet before the shooting so they look as similar as possible to the *Musulmannen*, as the terminally wasted, hopeless human ghosts were nicknamed by the other inmates who hadn't yet reached their state? And what about the hundreds of ex-tras supposed to mill around in the barracks and marching grounds and selection lines? How thin can one ask or demand of them to be-come for the ten or twenty dollars they get as a shooting day's fee? And say all this was done, say their wages were doubled and tripled—is a healthy person even capable of willingly starving him-self, so as to look like someone who'd been cruelly, systematically starved for weeks and months?

So even from this narrow aspect of physical appearance, any at-tempt at cinematic re-creation of the reality of the concentration camps is always doomed to failure and to belittling the real magni-tude of the Holocaust. The victims in the movie concentration camp, as thin and as decrepit as they manage to appear, will always look worlds better, stronger, and healthier than the real prisoners in the real German concentration camps, in the European reality of less than sixty years ago. To be convinced of this, all you have to do is look at the original still photographs and film footage taken when the camps were liberated in 1945.

In *Schindler's List*,[2] the Oscar-winning Holocaust drama that came before *Life Is Beautiful*, director Steven Spielberg tried to tackle this fundamental issue by intermingling, among the "normally" thin ac-tors, a few dreadfully thin extras who were supposed to provide the effect of extreme starvation characteristic to most concentration camp prisoners. In *Life Is Beautiful*, director Roberto Benigni did not attempt a similar brutal-diet re-creation like Spielberg's. In his film's concentration camp, people are just normally thin or of average weight.

And indeed, although both Spielberg and Benigni set out to con-cretize for their viewers the horrors of the Holocaust through a dramatized story taking place in a concentration camp, they took di-ametrically opposed approaches to the question of verisimilitude.

Spielberg located his film's story in an identifiable World War II concentration camp, Plaszow, near the Polish city of Krakow. It was there that the real events on which the film is based—the rescue of more than 1,000 of Plaszow's Jewish prisoners by their Sudeten-German employer, Oscar Schindler—indeed took place. Spielberg attempted to reproduce this camp and what went on there more or less accurately, within the medium's limitations. The result was a skillful and polished cinematic reproduction, problematic in its own way but not of our concern here. Benigni, conversely, located his film in a "generic" concentration camp—nameless, unspecific, fictionalized—a fantasy camp nowhere in particular, presumably representing all camps everywhere. Hence he "reproduced" his camp and what happens in it along broadly general lines, leaving large scope for the imagination.

Another "realism" problem both directors faced centered around the multitude of languages spoken by the prisoners, who were brought to the camps from countries all over Europe. As opposed to the visual reproduction problem, this one was solved by both directors in a similar fashion. Both the Germans and the Polish Jews in *Schindler's List*, conveniently for Spielberg and his American audience, speak fluent English. In *Life Is Beautiful*, Benigni separated the Italian Jews in his concentration camp from all the other Jews of Europe, or at least made the latter mute; thus the narrative develops, conveniently for Benigni and his Italian audience, mostly in Italian, mixed with a little German.

But the riot of languages was not, in reality, just a technical difficulty. This is spelled out in another book by Primo Levi, *Survival in Auschwitz*:

> The confusion of tongues is a fundamental component of the manner of living here: one is surrounded by a perpetual Babel, in which everyone shouts orders and threats in languages never heard before, and woe betide whoever fails to grasp the meaning. No one has time here, no one has patience, no one listens to you.[3]

And he adds, in *The Drowned and the Saved:*

> The greater part of the prisoners who did not understand German— that is, almost all the Italians—died during the first ten to fifteen days of their arrival: at first glance, from hunger, cold, fatigue, and disease; but after a more attentive examination, due to insufficient information.[4]

And, finally,

> For all of us survivors, who are not exactly polyglot, the first days in the *Lager* [camp] remain impressed in our memories like an out-of-focus and frenzied film, filled with a dreadful sound and fury signifying nothing: a hubbub of people without names or faces drowned in a continuous, deafening background noise from which, however, the human word did not surface. A black and gray film, with sound but not a talkie.[5]

And yet, even though these two important characteristics—the prisoners' physical appearance and their mixture of languages—clearly demonstrate the problematic nature of any attempt at a realistic reproduction of the Holocaust's external reality as a way of representing its horrors on the screen, they were not, in the final analysis, the central or most meaningful elements of concentration camp existence.

The one central, routine, inescapable, incomparably dominant fact of life in a concentration camp—the primary factor, unequaled in its significance—was death.

This central aspect, for a person living in our time and place, lucky enough to be leading a more or less "normal" life in more or less "normal" conditions, is especially hard to imagine. Life in a concentration camp was in fact a life inside death. It was led, as a matter of course, inside an organized valley of slaughter, an assembly line of death in which each and every person, jailer and prisoner alike, was a cog in a nonstop, systematic murder machine.

In the filmed concentration camp of *Schindler's List,* the death and the murder are indeed explicitly present on screen. But in the *Life Is Beautiful* camp, death is conspicuously absent. The film does not show, and therefore the viewers never see, even one instance of killing.

Yes, death is obliquely referred to. The film does present, here and there, talk of death and killing. One scene expressly mentions gas chambers, and in another there's a threat of a shot to the back of the neck. But in the film's visual reality, in the image that the film displays for the viewers—and the cinema is a visual medium, after all—no one dies, not to mention that no one is even seen being killed.

We could try guessing whether Roberto Benigni decided to do away with death in his concentration camp; that is, to hide it from the viewers, out of artistic or marketing considerations. Perhaps he thought that onscreen death (and especially of the particularly hor- rific nature—the mass, methodical, industrialized murder of mil- lions of innocent people—associated with the Nazi camps) might repel potential viewers of a film that is supposed, after all, to be a comedy. Possibly he had other motives. But these hypothetical con- siderations are irrelevant to the final, indisputable outcome: in the *Life Is Beautiful*–style concentration camp, death is invisible.

Indeed, in this respect, writer-director Benigni does to his viewers exactly what Guido, the character Benigni plays, does to his son in the film. In everything he says and does, in everything he chooses to either show the boy or to conceal from him—he keeps hiding the very presence of death in the concentration camp; that is, the actual fact of the extermination of the Jews in the Holocaust. But, at the same time, he does it to us as well, in everything he tells and does not tell us, in everything he does and does not show on screen.

And again, we must clearly distinguish between these two choices. The decision of the father, played by Benigni, to hide from his son the death occurring all around them isn't just perfectly legit- imate; it's the essence of the story Benigni wanted to tell his viewers. But the question remains: why did Benigni make such a point of hid- ing death not only from his screen son, but also—if not mainly— from his film's viewers?

He could conceivably tell the same story while we, the viewers, as opposed to the child in the film—from our different vantage point, which is essentially contemporary, more historically informed, ma- turer, and broader—are allowed to witness the surrounding death machine at work.

But Benigni, deliberately and consistently, chose to keep invisible the mass extermination—any instance of death, in fact—presumably taking place all around the core narrative he concocted. It is kept to- tally invisible, not only from his protagonist's son in the film, in the father's attempt, so we are made to believe, to save the child's life, but also from us, the audience, some fifty-odd years later.

This peculiar concealment is particularly striking in the scene of the killing of the father, near the end of the film. The German soldier, having caught the Jew trying to escape disguised as a woman in a futile attempt to find his wife among the women prisoners, is about to shoot Guido on the spot—that is, in front of the camera. But no. Right there appears his commander, who stops him, shouting in

German: "Halt! What are you doing? Not here, take him to the usual place."

And the German soldier duly obeys and takes Guido-Benigni on a rather long march that takes them past the son's hiding place, from where he peeks at his father who is walking like a clown, until they disappear behind a wall, which hides them from the camera—that is, from the viewers. Only there—off screen, out of our sight—does the German shoot the Jew, while we see nothing. It is only because immediately some shots are heard and then we see the soldier coming out from behind the wall alone that we are invited to infer, as we indeed do, that the Jewish father has been shot to death.

Relative to historical reality, this sequence, too, denies by implication the actual truth of the Holocaust. The official, legalized license to kill Jews—men, women, young, and old—right in public, with no need to hesitate or to seek any legal, moral, or other justification, at any time and place, for any excuse or for no excuse at all, was an integral part of the process of the Holocaust and its essence. The elimination of a Jew, officially branded as nonhuman, was a nonevent, especially in the concentration camps, where the Nazis had no need, as they sometimes had in other circumstances and places, to hide their actions in order to deceive popular opinion. This mindset became even more pronounced in the last days of the war, according to accounts of the few who somehow managed to survive the murderous frenzy of the "death marches" on which the Germans, on the eve of their defeat, took the prisoners still alive in the camps.

So again one wonders why the German commander orders his underling not to shoot the Jewish escapee right away, where he was caught. Is he ashamed of this action, or has he been abruptly seized by moral scruples that make it hard for him to watch a Jew being killed?

The answer, yet again, is elementary: it's a film. Therefore, the officer and the soldier do not unexpectedly act according to the dictates of their conscience, nor according to their commanders' orders. They act and behave as they are made to by the scriptwriter who conceived of and wrote them. Roberto Benigni (together with his co-scriptwriter, Vincenzo Cerami) conceived of and wrote them this way and made the commander tell the soldier not to shoot the Jew on the spot but to take the Jew away and shoot him off-camera, out of our sight. It was Benigni, not the commander or the soldier, who decided to kill the protagonist of his film this way—offscreen—and did. It isn't the father, played by Benigni, who hides his death from his son; it is his creator, Benigni himself, who hides from the viewers this particular death, and by implication the actuality of death in the concentration camp in general.

There is only one place in the film where Benigni does show, at least ostensibly, the mass organized extermination of the Jews. Fleetingly, he lets the viewers glimpse the results of the ongoing massacre in his film's concentration camp and, we may assume, in the concentration camps in general. This happens when Guido and his son lose their way in the mist while going back to their barrack from the dinner they participated in in the company of German officers and their children. Guido says to the child, who is asleep in his arms: "Where are we? I took a wrong turn, Giosue. Oh good—you're asleep. Pleasant dreams. Maybe it's really all a dream. Just a dream, Giosue."

Guido mumbles another sentence or two, fantasizing about a renewed family idyll with Dora, his beloved wife, including an imagined lovemaking session with her. Then the mist suddenly lifts, briefly. The father and the film's audience—but not the sleeping child—see a huge pile of corpses, filling the screen for a split second, then vanishing back into the fog.

This bluish, misty picture is so blurred, and disappears so quickly, that the viewers can hardly discern any details; many apparently do not even remember, at the end of the film, that it contained such an image at all.

Ostensibly, Benigni does at this point allow his viewers to see, even if for a brief second, the actual fact of mass murder in a German Holocaust camp. But we might as well notice that this whole scene, and particularly the pile of corpses as seen by the protagonist, is presented through a lens of fantasy. It is the only time this stylistic choice is made in the entire film, which is otherwise consummately realistic in its visual style. It is depicted as a kind of nightmarish hallucination rising in the mind of the tired, delirious Guido, lost in the mist and comforting his son—"Maybe it's really all a dream. Just a dream, Giosue"—and not a real pile of corpses that Guido actually sees, the kind of pile that was a horribly common sight in the camps, especially near the end of the war.

Aside from the father's off-camera execution at the end of the film and this one brief, nightmarish hallucination, no Jew is killed in Benigni's camp for the entire length of the film.

Moreover, for the entire film, no Jew is even beaten.

In the arrival scene, for instance, the German soldiers display quite remarkable politeness and courtesy: politeness and courtesy that, needless to say, are in stark contrast to the calculated brutality of the "reception" held for the new arrivals to the real concentration and extermination camps, meant to stun the victims and proactively prevent any possible resistance. In the film, this reception includes neither beatings, stripping, fumigating, nor shaving of the head (Benigni disregards historical fact and lets his inmates keep their full heads of hair for the whole duration of their camp stay). For the sake of comparison, let us consider Primo Levi's description in *The Drowned and the Saved*:

> The entire sinister ritual—varying from *Lager* to *Lager*, but basically similar—which accompanied the arrival: kicks and punches right away, often in the face; an orgy of orders screamed with true or simulated rage; complete nakedness after being stripped; the shaving off of one's hair; the outfitting in rags. It is difficult to say whether all these details were devised by some expert or methodically perfected on the basis of experience, but they certainly were willed and not casual: it was all staged, as was quite obvious.[6]

In the film, the women and the elderly are indeed separated in this scene from the others, and sent—as noted, with surprising politeness and courtesy—to another line, walking in a different, ominous direction; but it's never actually made clear what really happens to them. Guido's wife, Dora, who is put in the women's line, survives by the end of the film; hence not all of those sent in that direction were supposedly put to death.

Also missing is the rigid hierarchy of the prisoner society that developed in the camps, inspired and encouraged by the camps' German commanders and overseers. Benigni cancelled out the important middlemen function of the *Kapos*—those privileged prisoners, usually criminals, who were in actual charge of the brutal day-to-day routine. In *Survival in Auschwitz*, Primo Levi explains:

> We had soon learned that the guests of the *Lager* are divided into three categories: the criminals, the politicals and the Jews. All are clothed in stripes, all are *Häftlinge* [detainee], but the criminals wear a green triangle next to the number sewn on the jacket; the politicals wear a red triangle; and the Jews, who form the large majority, wear the Jewish

star, red and yellow. S.S. men exist but are few and outside the camp, and are seen relatively infrequently. Our effective masters in practice are the green triangles, who have a free hand over us.[7]

In Benigni's film, there are no *Kapos* or any acts of premeditated or random cruelty. The German officers, soldiers, and guards yell at the Jews, and that is presented as surely unpleasant, very insulting, and even frightening, but, throughout the entire film, none of them beat, abuse, humiliate, spit at, kick, whip, let loose bloodhounds at, or even lightly slap a single Jew.

In the *Life Is Beautiful* Nazi concentration camp, it's not only that the Jews are not being killed, but also that they never fall victim to any violence, not even incidentally. In reality, of course, according to Primo Levi, prisoners "took endless beatings."

This, then, is the film's vision: a violence-free concentration camp; a death-free Holocaust.

Strangely, this is exactly the claim of Holocaust deniers of all kinds and stripes, like the British David Irving and his ilk in other countries. They do not deny that detention camps of some sort, even "concentration camps," in fact existed. Neither do they deny that the Jews in those camps were made to do forced labor, even in harsh conditions. They do not even deny that many of the Jews imprisoned in the camps died from disease, exhaustion, and malnutrition.

What Holocaust deniers crucially deny is the one thing that made the Holocaust what it was: the fact that in some of those camps, Jews were systematically massacred as part of the workings of the gigantic mechanism instituted by the Nazi German superpower specifically toward this end, the extermination of all European Jews. That, they assert, is no more than a figment of a sick imagination or a "Jewish fabrication."

Hence, the image of a concentration camp in *Life Is Beautiful* and, by implication, its image of the Holocaust as a whole is startlingly, alarmingly reminiscent of the lying claims of Holocaust deniers.

Worse still: in its portrayal of the concentration camp and its proceedings, this film goes even further than the most orthodox of Holocaust deniers. Although some of them admit that acts of violence were committed in the camps, that prisoners were punished by beating, and that perhaps even sporadic killings on individual initiative occurred here and there, even such distasteful occurrences are absent from Benigni's camp. The Jews are neither killed nor tortured there. On the contrary, Benigni's Germans give them fair medical care and maybe even save their lives, as with the prisoner who is wounded in an accident and whose arm is duly stitched in the infirmary.

Indeed, *Life Is Beautiful*'s concentration camp not only doesn't look anything like the real German concentration camps, but it also looks kinder than contemporary detention camps for political or criminal detainees in some Third World countries, perhaps even kinder than camps for Third World illegal immigrants caught seeking work in certain Western countries.

Even prison life in the democratic United States, or at least certain aspects of it, as presented to cinema viewers worldwide through Hollywood's cameras seems worse than the conditions in Benigni's cinematic concentration camp. For instance, in *The Shawshank Redemption*,[8] whose story takes place in an American prison, the protagonist, a prisoner, must invest years of hard work and careful planning to slowly and cunningly overcome countless obstacles until he is able to gain a few seconds by himself in the prison's loudspeaker room, which he exploits to let his fellow inmates hear music from a phonograph.

In *Life Is Beautiful*, whose plot takes place in a Nazi concentration camp, the protagonist, a Jewish prisoner, walks effortlessly, without facing any obstacle, into the camp's loudspeaker room, from where he broadcasts to his heart's content a long message to his beloved wife who is also imprisoned in the camp. He then slips away without being caught or punished.

Based on this particular comparison, it seems that no intelligent viewer would find it hard to decide where he'd prefer to be imprisoned: in a tough, regular American prison or in a German concentration camp?

The prison camps in dictatorships, criminal prisons worldwide and the American ones in Hollywood's films, camps for Third World illegal immigrants, as well as Benigni's concentration camp—there is one thing in common to all these real and fictionalized institutions of detention and punishment that sets them apart from the German concentration and extermination camps of the 1930s and 1940s. Despite the harsh, even terrible conditions in most of them, including, in many cases, torture, sometimes to the point of death, one thing is absent from them. None of these places, terrible as each is in its own way, is meant or used for the organized, methodical extermination of the prisoners, their families, and millions of other innocent people, officially declared as *untermenchen,* subhumans, with no right to exist from the moment they are born. This was the exclusive distinction of the German death camps.

Compared to the German camps or to detention or labor camps in other dictatorships, Benigni's concentration camp isn't that bad; it's even pretty reasonable, albeit tough—one could almost say, Hitler's holiday camp.

A major key to demonstrating the profound misunderstanding or willful obscuring of the real nature of the Holocaust in the film lies in the scene sequence in which the prisoner child Giosue, Guido's son, is taken by mistake to dinner along with the children of the camp's commanding officers. The sequence starts with Guido-Benigni, during a camp medical checkup, recognizing the German physician as his old friend from before the war, when he was a waiter at a restaurant. The physician, Dr. Lessing, arranges for his old friend an easy job as a waiter in the camp's officers' mess. While working there, Guido sees a group of the officers' children playing hide-and-seek in the yard. An idea pops into his head. He runs to the barrack where Giosue is hiding, then takes him to where the children are playing to show little Giosue, who thought he was the only one his age in the camp, that he was wrong and there are other children left in camp. They're just hiding as part of the same game in which the father has convinced the son that all the people in the concentration camp are participating.

The father takes the child to a small metal hut outside in the yard and urges him to open it. Giosue opens the metal door and finds hiding behind it a boy who yells something in German. Giosue closes the door, and then the father explains that the boy inside the little hut has been hiding there for three weeks; he was ranked second in the game, but now they've eliminated him.

The two start on their way back to the barrack, but then a German woman attendant steps out and calls the children to dinner. All the children come out of their hiding places and go to her, but she spots Giosue too and calls him to come with her. Guido tells his son to go with the German woman but warns him not to say a single word; the viewers are thus given to understand that the father is afraid that the boy's language will give him away. Believing that this is all part of the game whose winner is going to get a tank as a prize, the boy swears to obey his father's command and goes with the attendant and the German children.

Guido returns to his work as a waiter, while his son, with no visible sign of discomfort, enjoys dinner in the next room with the German officers' children. But then, momentarily distracted, Giosue suddenly says to the German waiter serving him "Thank you" in Italian. As the astonished waiter rushes off to summon the attendant; Guido presents himself in front of the children and teaches them all to say "Thank you" in Italian, and so saves his son. At the end of the meal, the child drops his head on the table and falls asleep. His father later carries him in his arms back to their barrack.

A seemingly moving, heartwarming sequence. But for this to have happened in a concentration camp the way it happens in the film, all the participants should have been both blind and deaf, or at least completely lacking even a minimal ability of observation and discrimination to the point of being complete idiots.

The boy Giosue, the son of Guido-Benigni, a six-year-old child imprisoned in a German concentration camp, sees German children, sons and daughters of the camp's officers and their wives, and doesn't realize that they are not prisoners like him. Not even when they speak to him in German. Even if he doesn't know the name of this language, he must surely know—because he had already heard it in earlier scenes—that it is the one spoken by the "bad guys" in the game that his father convinced him they were taking part in (the father even warns him that "they talk so weird, you can't understand a thing"). But no—the child understands nothing and doesn't even notice the difference between him and the other children.

On the other hand, none of the Germans who come in contact with Giosue in this sequence—the attendant, the whole group of children, the officer who reproaches them for the noise they make, the waiter serving them—notices that this boy is different from the others, that he is a prisoner and not the son of a German officer.

In order to create an excuse in the plot for this mistake to be remotely plausible, the scriptwriters let rain fall the night before. This supposedly turned the earth muddy, and thus—according to the script, at least, because in the film itself we don't get to see even a touch of mud in this scene—this error is made possible. The German children are supposed to get dirty, too, while playing hide and seek, and that is why they can't tell the difference, and neither can the German attendant, who just reproaches the prisoner boy for being "the dirtiest of all."

Which is to say: the only difference between a child imprisoned in a concentration camp and the children of the officers of the camp is, allegedly, that the prisoner child is a little dirtier. A few imaginary mudstains unmake the fundamental differences—physical, psychological, existential—between the victim and the children of his persecutors and torturers.

Actually, in the film, even this degree-of-dirtiness difference isn't very detectable. The boy-prisoner looks surprisingly neat and tidy, not only in these scenes but throughout the film. His hair is combed; his face is clean; he doesn't scratch for lice; his clothes aren't torn and tattered; and his eyes are not sunken in his skull.

Neither is the way this presumably starved boy eats his food much different, as the film shows it, from the way the other children eat theirs. His father does warn him to "eat slowly or you'll be sick," but this warning seems unnecessary and the child has no trouble heeding it.

And indeed, no one notices anything strange about Giosue's behavior, as no one ever wonders about his presence. Only when he accidentally speaks a word in Italian does he raise any suspicion, and that, too, is dispelled quite quickly and easily.

Again, during this entire sequence, purportedly taking place in a concentration camp, no one notices any difference between a group of free, well-fed, pampered children of the German camp officers and a prisoner child, starved for weeks and maybe months, who, moreover, for this whole time hasn't taken a single bath or changed his clothes; a child who is living in constant hiding and deep fear (even if he thinks it's just a part of some game).

This kind of mistaken identity was simply impossible in a real concentration camp, and therefore this sequence too denies the reality of the Holocaust. This is because if there were even a slight possibility for someone who lived in a concentration camp—whether prisoner or guard—to err and not notice immediately, at a glance, without hesitation, the abysmal difference between a prisoner-victim child and the children of his German jailers, it logically follows that the difference between the jailers' children's appearance and condition and those of the prisoners' children (if they weren't murdered yet) was negligible at worst, or practically nonexistent. So what went on in those concentration camps wasn't perhaps that terrible after all.

And it should again be remembered, in this context as well, that this is a film. Hence the lack of ability to draw a distinction—both visual and psychological—between the persecuted child and the children of his persecutors and oppressors isn't a fault of the German attendant or officer, the German waiter, or the German officer's children. The lack of ability to tell them apart is solely that of the film's creator. It is Benigni who does not differentiate between the two classes of children he brings together: those who were branded as subhuman and treated accordingly—and those who must have known that they and their parents were members of a master race and as such were forbidden nothing. The creator of this film does not understand and thus obscures the fundamental nature of the Holocaust.

Are these misunderstandings, examples of lack of discrimination, and evasions apparent throughout the film insignificant, a matter of silly, meaningless coincidence? Or is there some pattern, logic, and method at work here—whether consciously or not—adding up to a whole, significant statement?

For, strangely but unmistakably, the way the film—created by a European Christian at the end of the twentieth century—portrays the extermination of European Jews appears to have much in common with the way the extermination was actually received, fifty years earlier, by the vast majority of European Christians.

In the film, Jews aren't murdered—at worst, they just go away and disappear. This, of course, was the most comfortable way for the Christian neighbors of the Jews, in most European countries, to look at (or, to be precise, not look at), imagine, and describe what happened during the days of the Holocaust itself. We really don't know what happened, so many of them said after the war; it's just that suddenly, one fine morning, the Jews went away and never came back; they were just gone.

NOTES

1. Primo Levi, *The Drowned and the Saved* (*I sommersi e i salvati*), trans. Raymond Rosenthal (New York: Vintage Books, 1989).

2. *Schindler's List*, script: Steven Zaillian, based on a novel by Thomas Kenealy, director: Steven Spielberg, United States 1993.

3. Primo Levi, *Survival in Auschwitz: The Nazi Assault on Humanity* (*Se questo é un uomo*), trans. Stuart Woolf (New York: Touchstone Books, 1995).

4. Levi, *The Drowned and the Saved.*
5. Levi, *The Drowned and the Saved.*
6. Levi, *The Drowned and the Saved.*
7. Levi, *Survival in Auschwitz.*
8. *The Shawshank Redemption,* script: Frank Darabont, based on the novel by Stephen King, director: Frank Darabont, United States 1994.

Chapter 2

Reality as Fairy Tale

Here and there, some of the film's rare detractors pointed to the problematic aspects of *Life Is Beautiful* discussed in the last chapter, namely, that Benigni's concentration camp is too mild a place to be even remotely comparable to the real camps, and that mass extermination and indeed death itself are conspicuously absent from his film in a way dismayingly reminiscent of some of the ugliest slanders of Holocaust deniers. Though these dissenting voices were more or less drowned in the great chorus of love and admiration that greeted *Life Is Beautiful* everywhere it was screened, there were also some attempts to counter this particular critique of the film with seemingly pertinent objections. A reply to these objections may therefore be in order here, before I go on to develop my wider argument about the message of the film as a whole.

One common objection I ran into has been that the camp in the film isn't a "concentration camp" at all, just a "labor camp," and that's why they don't kill any prisoners in it and there is no death on screen.

Well, first, if this really is just an "innocent" labor camp and not a monstrous concentration camp, the whole of the film's plot becomes quite pointless. For why exactly does the father have to protect his son by making up that complicated story about the game and gaining points to win a tank if there's no need to, since the child is not actually in mortal danger at all?

Second, in the script written by Benigni and his cowriter, Vincenzo Cerami—in the original Italian as well as in the Hebrew and English translations—the place to which the father and son are taken and in which the game is being played is expressly designated a "Concentration Camp."

Another objection of the same kind I've come across in the film's defense was that the camp is not located in Poland, where mass extermination did take place, but in Italy, where prisoners were treated much more humanely. So, once again, assuming this was the case, in such a humane camp the film's plot would lose its logic and its psychological justification, since Guido, the father, would have no reason to make up the tank game.

Nevertheless, these objections do raise a more general question, about which there is at least some degree of confusion for those unfamiliar with the specific historical terms—which probably means the absolute majority of the tens of millions who saw *Life Is Beautiful*: what did the term "concentration camp" mean, literally and in practice, in the European reality of World War II? And what is the connection, if any, between that and the camp as presented in the film?

"Concentration camp" is English for the German term *Konzentrationslager*, used by the Nazis to designate "camps in which persons are imprisoned without regard to the accepted norms of arrest and detention"—as explained in *The Encyclopedia of the Holocaust*.[1]

By this narrow definition, there were indeed concentration camps in Italy as well. I further quote from that basic, reliable source:

On the eve of Italy's entry into the war (June 10, 1940) . . . [there were] mass arrests of the foreign nationals among the Jews who had not complied with the expulsion order issued in 1938. Men, women and children were thrown into jail with no charges brought against them and were often held under appalling conditions. . . . On September 4, the Ministry of the Interior ordered forty-three concentration camps to be established, for the imprisonment of enemy aliens and of Italians suspected of subversive activities. Among the prisoners in these camps were thousands of Jews who were foreign nationals or stateless persons, and 200 Italian Jews who were known to oppose the Fascist regime.[2]

But the encyclopedia goes on to clarify,

With respect to the prisoners' physical safety and their living conditions, there was no comparison between the concentration camps in Italy and those set up by the Nazis in Germany and in the countries they occupied. In the Italian concentration camps, families lived together; there were schools for the children and a broad program of social welfare and cultural activities. For the most part, the work imposed on the prisoners involved only services required for the camp itself.[3]

This description is markedly different from the camp life in *Life Is Beautiful*. It is also incompatible with the film's plot, since the lives of Jews held in the Italian camps were not in danger at that time and those camps' guards were Italians, not Germans.

Furthermore, historically, by the time Guido and Giosue were arrested according to the film, conditions in the part of Italy where Arezzo, their hometown, is located had completely changed.

Following the surrender of Italy's Fascist government on September 8, 1943, to the Allies, the Germans directly occupied most of Italy, from Naples northward, and immediately applied the "Final Solution" to Jews in the occupied area. According to the *Encyclopedia*, "The Jews were hunted down mercilessly . . . [and] deported to extermination camps, mainly to Auschwitz."[4] Primo Levi, incidentally, was one of those deportees.

It bears repeating here that the term "concentration camp"—in the German-Jewish context—is usually perceived in the popular mind, especially that of post–World War II generations both in Israel and in other countries, not as designating a "concentration camp" by its original, specific, Nazi-bureaucratic (and therefore, encyclopedic-historic) definition. It is usually construed as referring to one of the special camps constructed on occupied Polish soil whose sole aim was the murder of the Jewish people. Benigni, at least at first glance, seems to have understood the term and used it according to this popular meaning.

It is worthwhile, therefore, to elaborate a little on this matter, in order to sort out the terms that tend to get mixed up. Historically, based on the German Nazi bureaucracy's own definitions, there were actually three kinds of camps:

1. Concentration camps, or *Konzentrationslager*, where Jews from all over Europe, Gypsies, Soviet POWs, political prisoners opposing the Nazi regime, and other "undesirables" were concentrated and used as forced laborers, many to the point of death. These were mostly camps on German soil,

some of which were built by the Nazis before the war, such as Buchenwald, Dachau, Bergen-Belsen, and many others, but camps of this kind also existed in Austria, Estonia, Lithuania, Latvia, Yugoslavia, and Poland.

2. Extermination camps, *Vernichtungslager* in German, were

> Nazi camps in occupied Poland in which a huge number of Jews were killed, as part of the "Final Solution of the Jewish question in Europe." These camps had a single goal: the blanket murder of the Jews, irrespective of age or sex. In contrast to the procedure at other camps, no *Selektionen* took place (with some exception in Auschwitz-Birkenau); everyone brought to an extermination camp, including persons fit for work, was murdered. For this reason, such camps have sometimes been called "death factories."

There were very few places, all of them in Poland, compatible with this specific definition: Chelmno, Belzec, Sobibor, and Treblinka.

3. Sites that were both concentration and extermination camps also operated on Polish soil. There were two of these: Majdanek, in eastern Poland; and, chiefly, Auschwitz-Birkenau, a combined concentration, labor, and extermination camp, in southwestern Poland, "both the most extensive of some two thousand Nazi concentration and forced-labor camps, and the largest camp at which Jews were exterminated by means of poison gas."[5]

As a matter of historical fact, most Italian Jews captured by the Germans were sent to Auschwitz-Birkenau in Poland, and the rest were sent to Ravensbruck and Bergen-Belsen in Germany.

Which of these camps does Benigni depict in his film? The camp part of the film was reportedly shot on location in a deserted, former factory in Italy, which explains why the physical appearance of this camp and its surrounding landscape bear no resemblance to those of any real, historical camp. Because the film does not spell out the camp's name or definite location, we can only try to identify the characteristics of the anonymous concentration camp in *Life Is Beautiful*, and maybe infer from them the actual historical camp where the story presumably takes place.

The distinguishing features of the camp as shown in the film are as follows:

1. All prisoners, or at least all those who speak in the film, are Italians.
2. The prisoners are forced to labor in a nearby industrial facility.
3. Men and women are separated in different subcamps.
4. One of the female inmates says that the showers where some of the women are taken are in reality gas chambers.
5. Guido tells his son that the Germans have written (that is, tattooed) his prisoner number on his forearm.

And so, disregarding the first item—the fact that all the prisoners are Italian, assuming that this was a choice made for the sake of mere cinematic convenience—the only camp that the film could be depicting is Auschwitz-Birkenau. It was the only camp that had all the major features of the one in the film: the forced labor in factories erected nearby; the separate subcamps for men and women; the combined functions that the camp served—a "regular" concentration camp, whose inmates were used as forced laborers, as well as a camp for the extermination by gassing of transports of Jews brought from all over Europe for this purpose only, their immediate murder, and not for the intention of imprisoning them as regular inmates; and especially the numbers routinely tattooed on prisoners' forearms, a practice that was peculiar to Auschwitz-Birkenau alone.

As for the other camps to which Italian Jews were deported, Bergen-Belsen didn't have a gas chamber, whereas Ravensbruck, which did have a single gas chamber, was a women-only camp. When this historical information is added to the equation, deducing that the film's concentration camp could only be Auschwitz-Birkenau becomes even more compelling.

But if, according to both historical fact and narrative logic, this camp is likely to be Auschwitz-Birkenau, why didn't Benigni call a spade a spade? Why did he make such a point of concealing the precise identity of the camp in his film? Were his reasons economical, that is, he wanted to save his production the vast funds required for the exact replication of Auschwitz? Was it just a matter of sloppiness, a careless disregard for historical truth? Or would it hurt the story in any way had the camp been a particular rather than a generic one? Was the decision to obscure the camp's identity due to an ideology of some kind or a message that Benigni wished to convey?

What did Benigni actually gain from hiding the particular identity of Auschwitz-Birkenau and turning it into a nameless, unspecific

concentration camp—even though it has some very specific distinguishing features?

There are two things that he gained, both stemming from two essential differences between the two camps: the real one and the one
in the film. First, in Auschwitz-Birkenau, a nonstop, huge massacre
of Jews went on, but in his own nameless cinematic camp no Jews
are seen being killed. Second, the USSR's Red Army liberated the
real Auschwitz-Birkenau, whereas Benigni's fake concentration
camp is liberated by the U.S. Army.

So, turning the Auschwitz-Birkenau concentration and extermination camp into the film's anonymous camp serves two purposes:

1. To play down and conceal, if not outright deny, the mass murder
   of Jews in the Holocaust by visually presenting the concentration
   camps, Auschwitz included, as not-so-bad places overall, in
   which, despite some talk hinting at a gas shower, no one was actually killed, except maybe for a single Italian Jew.
2. To realize the highest dream of an Oscar, the glorious top
   award of the American and international industry of illusions.
   Had Benigni been loyal to historical truth, he wouldn't have
   been able to show an American soldier arriving in a tank to free
   the child from the concentration camp at the end of the film. He
   would have been forced to let a Soviet soldier, of all creatures—
   a Russian-speaking communist, God forbid—bring about salvation, freedom, and happiness, but not the Oscar.

Benigni himself, in a foreword to the original script published in
book form in Italy, explains his decision to shoot his film in an
unidentified concentration camp by arguing that "the camp isn't a
particular concentration camp" but that "it represents all concentration camps in the world, at all times."[6]

The logic behind this argument seems somewhat puzzling. If, as
Benigni implies, his purpose is truly to warn the world against the
danger of concentration camps in general, can't this specific concentration camp, Auschwitz-Birkenau, indeed the largest and most horrific of them all, represent the world's concentration camps?
Can they only be represented by a unspecific, sugar-coated, and
"improved" concentration camp? Is the Auschwitz-Birkenau con-
centration-extermination camp—at which, according to the most
conservative, minimum estimate, close to a million people were

murdered in gas chambers, in addition to the tens of thousands murdered there by shooting, physical torture, lethal injections, and atrocious "medical experiments," or who died of disease and starvation—somehow less of a warning to humanity than Benigni's own invention of a fake, cute, deathless concentration camp?

Let's suppose, for the sake of the argument, that there indeed existed and still exist, in other times and places, camps just like those in which the Germans gathered Jews and Gypsies from all over Europe to exterminate them. If so, these camps, too, would have mass extermination going on in them, so Benigni should have somehow shown that fact in his "representative" concentration camp. But if those other concentration camps he talks about are not exactly like the German camps where industrialized massacre took place, then they may very well be "prison camps," "reeducation camps," or Soviet-style "gulags," but not German concentration or extermination camps. By showing in his film a German concentration camp without mass organized murder, Benigni dilutes and obscures the meaning of the concept, and thus, again, obscures and belittles the Holocaust.

Another objection I've heard was that *Life Is Beautiful* tells a real-life story—there really was such a father and son, who went through exactly what happens in the film; therefore, the tale as told is indisputable.

Even if this claim were true, it would not stand up in point of principle. Any story told by artistic means, even if based on real events, is always a made-up story in the sense that it isn't rendered to us "as is" straight from reality but is reconstructed and processed in one way or another, through various choices made by its narrator from among many storytelling alternatives. Hence the choice of manner in which it is narrated and presented is always open to dispute.

A more common objection claims the opposite—that the film doesn't pretend to tell a real story at all but is meant to be understood as a fable, a mere fairy tale. Therefore, even if it just so happens that this particular fairy tale uses the Holocaust for a backdrop, there is no point in looking for the truth of the Holocaust in it, much like one cannot expect the forest in which Red Riding Hood meets the wolf on her way to see Grandma to fulfill some strict criteria of a "realistic" forest.

The "fable" claim exists, at least ostensibly, in the film itself, in the words of the narrator (who can, from the context, be surmised to be the grown-up Giosue), heard in voiceover at the start of the film. The exact definition the narrator uses, that is, the word that Benigni put in his mouth to describe the nature of the story the film is about to tell, is the Italian word *favola*. The narrator says: "This is a simple story but not an easy one to tell. Like a fable, there is sorrow, and like a fable, it is full of wonder and happiness."

This introduction by a narrator, as well as his closing remarks at the end of the film—and his unseen character in general—did not exist in the original script. They were added at a later stage, proba-bly after the film's completion. But similar words by Benigni himself appear in the foreword to the book of the original script, in Italian: "This film is a fantasy, almost science fiction, a fable which has noth-ing realistic or neo-realistic in it, or anything taken from reality."[5]

The Italian word *favola* originates from the Latin *fabula,* and its modern Italian meaning may be, but isn't necessarily, "fairy tale" (as it was translated in the film's Hebrew subtitles). Like its English counterpart, "fable," this Italian word can have one of three princi-pal meanings: a parable, a fairy tale, or a fiction (it also has some other, less common, and more archaic meanings, one of which is "falsity").

Favola, therefore, may be a parable, an allegorical story with a moral lesson to it. And indeed, if this was the intention, then even by its name—before we find out what the allegory is about—the film fulfills the necessary criterion, since it declares at the outset that it means to teach us a lesson, namely, that *Life Is Beautiful.*

So *Life Is Beautiful* is certainly a parable. But is it a fairy tale?

A fairy tale is a story whose primary premise is our unequivocal knowledge that it didn't and couldn't occur in reality, that is, in any concrete or known time and place. As the classical opening of fairy tales goes, it all took place "a long time ago in a faraway land," in other words, what you are about to hear never was; not in our place, not here, not now, not in any known reality; only far, far away, a long, long time ago, somewhere within the realm of imagination.

Interpreting Benigni's use of the term *favola* as meaning that *Life Is Beautiful* is a fairy tale as it is commonly understood fails even the minimum test of the definition. Italian Fascism, German Nazism, World War II, and the extermination of Europe's Jews—all these were not part of an imaginary Brothers Grimm fairy tale that happened "a long time ago in a faraway land." They took place in reality, not that many years ago, in concrete, recognizable places in Europe, and not a few people who had been there are still alive among us and can testify to the authenticity of those events.

Thus, defining *Life Is Beautiful* as a fairy tale is tantamount in a sense to an attempt to turn historical reality, including the murder of the Jewish people, into a figment of the imagination, a fable that never was.

And in fact, the film's opening remarks are voiced over the hazy image of the father wandering in the mist with his son in his arms, taken from the scene that will appear toward the end of the film, in which Guido will half-see, half-hallucinate the pile of corpses—as if to impress on us that it is nothing more than a delusion or a nightmare that never really happened.

On the other hand, if we take *favola* to mean (realistic) "fiction"—a story that, even though fictitious, takes place against a backdrop of a recognizable, known reality—then *Life Is Beautiful* does fulfill the requirements.

But this interpretation, too, has been sometimes enlisted to justify the sugar-coating and diminishing of the Holocaust in the film. Some have claimed that *Life Is Beautiful* does not aspire to be a realistic film, a documentary, or historically accurate. It is simply a love story (between father and son, husband and wife, and child and mother) unfolding against the backdrop of the Holocaust. Being a mere backdrop, the Holocaust is not so important here that we should pettily nag the writer-director with nitpicking minutiae concerning the way he presents it in his film.

True, this isn't a historical or documentary film in the sense that it doesn't use cinematic tools to re-create, as accurately as possible, real past events. But *Life Is Beautiful* is a realistic film. That is to say, it is set, for all intents and purposes except for the extermination of Jews, in the historical reality of World War II in Europe.

Documentary or historical films tell stories or recreate events that happened in reality. All other realistic films are fiction by definition, telling tales and relating events that didn't necessarily happen but that could have happened in reality, one way or the other. *Life Is Beautiful,* therefore, largely falls under the definition of realistic fiction.

That the events described in it didn't really happen makes *Life Is Beautiful* neither a fairy tale nor a fantasy, nor an unrealistic film. By definition, events described in any nonhistorical, nondocumentary film didn't really happen. Or is each and every film that tells a fictional story a fairy tale?

Let's look, for instance, at *Titanic*,[7] a film similar in this respect to *Life Is Beautiful*. It, too, tells a made-up love story against the backdrop of a concrete, historical event—the sinking of the great ship in *Titanic*, the Jewish Holocaust in *Life Is Beautiful*.

Is *Titanic*, then, not a realistic film?

The only essential difference between the way the two films tell their respective stories is that in *Titanic* there is no attempt to visually conceal or in any way obscure the reality of the historical event against which the fictional love story unfolds. The film spares the viewers none of the disastrous truth of the ship's sinking. *Life Is Beautiful*, conversely, shows none of the disastrous truth of the extermination of the Jewish people. It coyly hides it.

When it comes to other background details, on the other hand, Benigni goes to great lengths, both as scriptwriter and director, to make these look as concrete and realistic as possible.

The car that Guido and his friend Ferruccio are traveling in at the beginning of the film is an actual Fiat Ballila (named after the Fascist youth movement)—the very model manufactured at the time the film's story takes place. The flags raised by the countrymen waiting for the king are the actual flags used in prewar Italy. The clothes and uniforms worn by the actors are exact replicas of those worn during the period. In the scenes taking place after the German occupation of northern Italy, Benigni made sure to show German soldiers marching through the city, and he surrounded the statues and public buildings with sandbags, the way it really was at the time in that area. Benigni reproduced the train going to the concentration camp with remarkable accuracy. The concentration camp's soldiers' and officers' uniforms and their ranks were replicated realistically. The prisoners' uniforms are also quite similar to those worn in real German concentration camps. The markings on them are different, though, from the real historic ones; the significance of this difference will be discussed later.

That is, Benigni carefully, painstakingly recreated, or attempted to recreate, almost every factual detail so as to achieve a nearly documentary realism. Except for one central omission. Precisely at the point where the film is supposed to be dealing directly with the minor detail of the extermination of the Jews, the strict regard to detail and exact verisimilitude suddenly stops. The brutality, the degrada-tion, the abuse, the organized murder just evaporate. At this precise stage, the film turns from a more or less realistic one into an outright fantasy, casually switching from an appearance of almost documen-tary realism to the inventiveness of a fairy tale, from accuracy in his-torical fact to what Benigni dubs "science fiction."

Some claimed in the film's defense that it was not really necessary, and indeed would be superfluous, to attempt to show in any direct way the horrors of the concentration camps, since "everybody knows anyway what went on there."

This is simply nonsense. It is not only that not "everybody knows what went on there," but also that most people—including, pre-sumably, a large part of those who saw and liked *Life Is Beautiful*—are very far from having any real knowledge of what went on there. The average person's knowledge, as far as it exists, is usually partial and quite inaccurate. Just one random statistical example: in a poll conducted in Germany and France among young adults between the ages 14–18, the results of which were published in early 2000 in the French weekly *Nouvel Observateur*,[8] 76 percent of the French youngsters and 65 percent of the German ones couldn't answer the question, "What was the Holocaust?" About half of the young Ger-mans knew that "it was something to do with the extermination of Jews," but only 13 percent of their French counterparts knew even that.

We should remember here that in World War II, a large part of French Jewry was expelled to Nazi camps by the local police, by official order of the Vichy government—the French collaborator regime—and that Germany was the country that initiated the ex-termination and carried it out. What, then, would be the results of a similar poll in countries that do not have a direct historical con-nection to the events?

Moreover, even if we accepted the assertion that "everybody knows anyway what went on there" as pure scientific fact, proven beyond any possible doubt, we would still have to ask: why, out of all the countless things that people "know anyway," did Benigni choose not to show this specific detail—the extermination of the Jews?

Benigni himself, in the foreword to his and Cerami's script, ex-plains why he chose to show a generic, unspecific concentration camp in his film. "And who said these horrors are unique to the

Nazis?" he asks, and answers: "The problem is that these horrors could always repeat themselves. They repeated themselves only recently, in Bosnia, for instance."

Here Benigni casually disproves the claim that "everybody knows." His own words are proof that even the creator of this film doesn't realize the essential difference between "the Holocaust"— the premeditated, organized, and methodical extermination of millions in Europe during World War II, after years of propaganda and deliberate ideological, legal, and bureaucratic preparation—and the atrocities mutually inflicted by opposing armies and peoples during armed conflicts.

Do we need a reminder that in every war since time began, atrocities, massacres, pillage, rape, and abuse have been and still are being committed? It's part of the nature of war, part of human nature itself. Civilian populations suffer great harm; whole villages are wiped out and their inhabitants slaughtered; women are raped, men executed, and children butchered. Almost every conqueror who has the opportunity commits these and similar acts, whether on a larger or a smaller scale, against the defeated enemy. The propensity toward hideous war crimes is not particular to certain tribes or peoples; it is sadly common to all peoples in wartime circumstances. The European colonialists—English, French, Italian, Spanish, Portuguese, and others—who all thought of themselves as belonging to a higher, merciful, Christian civilization did it wherever they went—in Asia, in Africa, and in America. The Germans did it to the conquered peoples of Europe during World War II. The Russians did it in their turn to the Germans. Americans did such things in Vietnam. The Serbs did it to the Albanians in Kosovo, and when the war turned their way, the Albanians did it to the Serbs. And it did happen in Bosnia, too, just as Benigni pointed out. Everyone does it, all the time, at any place where the rules of civilized society fall apart and circumstances are created that allow for the satisfaction of certain human urges. Aggressiveness and cruelty are an integral part of war.

However, no state of war ever existed between the Germans and the Jews in any recognized meaning of the term. The Jews did not have, during the 1930s and 1940s, in Europe or anywhere else, a state or an autonomous territorial entity that the Germans could have wanted to conquer; and, of course, they didn't have any kind of military force against which the Germans could wage war. The

Jews were declared an enemy while being unarmed, defenseless citizens of Germany itself and scattered throughout the countries of conquered Europe, where they had been living for many generations.

Historians might well debate the question of whether the murder of Jews in the Holocaust is comparable to the extermination of over a million Cambodians by the Pol Pot regime in the 1970s, or to the tens of millions of Russians and Chinese murdered in their own countries by the tyrannical regimes of Stalin and Mao respectively. These weren't, after all, spontaneous massacres—or even organized ones—committed in the madness of war, but methodical, continuous mass exterminations of civilian populations, initiated and presided over by evil regimes that established monstrous detention camps for their own citizens in the name of a declared ideology. In this respect, they really were more similar to the Holocaust than the sporadic wartime slaughters inflicted by states and peoples, whether by tyrannical regimes or by the armies of democracies.

I tend to agree with those who believe that there is, nevertheless, a difference between the crime committed against the Jews of Europe and the other horrors we have witnessed in recent generations, including recently in Rwanda, where hundreds of thousands of Tutsis were systematically slaughtered by the Hutu government's forces. All of them, horribly, qualify for the label "genocide" as defined by the UN General Assembly: "A denial of the right of existence of entire human groups," which was declared "a crime under international law."[9]

The difference, needless to say, does not lie in the extent of the cruelty of the crime or the number of its victims. There is no way and no moral justification whatsoever to make any kind of comparison between this suffering or that suffering, this or that terror, this or that brutality. A murder is a murder is a murder, whether the victim is a single human being or an entire people. The difference is, anyway, not one of quantity but of quality.

The extermination of the Jews was committed in an organized, methodical manner by the best available technical means of a modern superpower whose various systems and technological capabilities were all mobilized for this purpose over an extended period of time, after declaring total war on a certain part of its own population and of the civilian populations of countries it occupied. The Jews' property was appropriated, and their legal rights as citizens

and human beings were gradually abolished. This regime attempted to destroy all traces of their culture, ultimately trying to
exterminate them to the last individual, from newborn baby to the
aged, with the aim of completely wiping the group to which they
belonged off the face of the earth.

The British never wished to annihilate the people of India; the
Italians never wished to annihilate the Ethiopians; the Germans
never wished to annihilate the French; the French never wished to
annihilate the Algerians; the Americans never wished to annihilate
the Vietnamese; and so on and so forth, up to the Serbs who
wished to expel the Albanians from Kosovo and the Albanians
who wished in their turn to expel the Serbs—expel, not annihilate.
The professed and practical aims of the wars in which these and
other countries committed acts of slaughter throughout history
was to enslave those other peoples, to control their territories, or
even to exile them from them. To enslave and to exile, but not annihilate. Even the massacres of the Stalin, Mao, and Pol Pot
regimes were committed within the conceptual framework of
"class struggle"—as a cruel, demented exercise in social engineer-
ing in which the communist tyrants believed and professed that
they were "rebuilding society from the bottom up" and "creating a
new man." Those who were designated "class enemies" were brutally persecuted and mass murdered, but they were never classified as biologically "subhuman," as beings whose unforgivable
crime was the fact of having been born. Even in those terrible
regimes there was a basic assumption, as it were, that any person
is capable of being "reeducated" and made to conform, by force if
need be, to the demands of the regime's favored utopia and so become a "useful citizen" in it.

The extermination of the Jews was essentially different from all of
these on one main point: its totality. The Jews did not have even a
theoretical hope of escape or refuge. From the outset, their persecution by the Nazi regime wasn't aimed at defeating or controlling
them or at conquering any territory, which they didn't have anyway. It was not aimed at merely frightening and subduing them,
making religious converts out of them, or reeducating them by
changing their class consciousness, their lifestyle, or their behavior
in order to make them conform to life as dictated by some "ideals"
dear to the ruling regime. They were declared biological enemies,
pure and simple; nothing less than their physical extermination, to

the very last one of them, was the unavoidable conclusion and the consistent and stated aim of the war against them. As far as the German Third Reich was concerned, each and every Jew in the world, of every age and condition, no matter who or what they were, what opinions they held, and what they had or had not done for or against the state was simply sentenced to death by their very classification as Jews.

Primo Levi, in his book *The Drowned and the Saved*, considers a broad historical overview of the atrocities visited by human beings against their fellow humans, and reaches the conclusion that

> notwithstanding the horror of Hiroshima and Nagasaki, the shame of the Gulags, the useless and bloody Vietnam War, the Cambodian self-genocide, the *desaparecidos* of Argentina, and the many atrocities and stupid wars we have seen since, the Nazi concentration camp system still remains a *unicum*, both in its extent and its quality. At no other place or time has one seen a phenomenon so unexpected and so complex: never have so many human lives been extinguished in so short a time, and with so lucid a combination of technological ingenuity, fanaticism, and cruelty.

All these makes us again wonder: does Roberto Benigni really not know, or not understand, the difference between what happened in Auschwitz and what happened in Bosnia?

I don't know the answer, but I feel it important to reiterate: I am not trying to say that Benigni's film was conceived out of some conscious, malicious intent to belittle the crime committed against the Jews. I neither claim nor believe that he just said to himself, "I'm going to make a film that will deny the real nature of the Holocaust" or that he had been instructed to make such a film by some nonexistent "elders of the Vatican" cabal.

It's perfectly clear to me that this film isn't the result of conspiracy. Things don't work that way, and works of art aren't conceived that way, not in this case nor in general. Works of art and entertainment, including films, originate in and are born of their creators' subconscious.

Therefore, this book is not about Benigni's intentions, which cannot be known for certain anyway, but about their manifest results in the script he wrote and the film he created. From them, it tries to decipher the deep, probably unconscious, and hence, in my opinion, real message of the film Benigni made.

NOTES

1. Israel Gutman, chief ed., *The Encyclopedia of the Holocaust* (London: Collier Macmillan, 1990).

2. Gutman, *The Encyclopedia of the Holocaust.*

3. Gutman, *The Encyclopedia of the Holocaust.*

4. Gutman, *The Encyclopedia of the Holocaust.*

5. Gutman, *The Encyclpedia of the Hoocaust.*

6. Roberto Benigni and Vincenzo Cerami, *La vita é bella* (Turin, Italy: Einaudi, 1998)

7. *Titanic,* script and director: James Cameron, United States 1997.

8. *Nouvel Observateur* No. 1839, as quoted in *Haaretz Daily,* February 7, 2000.

9. Resolution 260, based on the general assembly declaration of December 11, 1946.

Chapter 3

See No Evil, Hear No Evil

Every allegory has a moral lesson to impart—the enlightening wisdom that the readers, or in this case the viewers, are supposed to gain from the story or the film, and hopefully apply to their own lives. What lesson is *Life Is Beautiful* trying to teach us?

There seems to be more than one such lesson. There is the obvious, "official" lesson as it were, learned by the first-person narrator, the adult Giosue, from what he went through as a child in the concentration camp—that is, the conclusion put in his mouth by scriptwriter Benigni (and his cowriter Cerami), which is to be found in the name of the film. It is a positive, optimistic, albeit somewhat childish moral lesson, so easy to embrace: "Despite all its difficulties, and even facing its greatest horrors, life is still good, beautiful, and worth living."

This or any other lesson can be learned, of course, only by the survivors. Only they, naturally, have the luxury of pronouncing life "beautiful" or complaining that "life is boring" or even crying out that "life is terrible." To the dead, life is not beautiful; neither is it ugly or terrible. They make no pronouncements, don't complain, and don't cry. The dead have no life to draw lessons from. They are dead.

And indeed, in the film, too, the verdict that "life is beautiful" is not reached by Guido, who dies in the concentration camp, but by his survivors—Giosue and Dora.

In the same spirit, the film aspires to teach us—seemingly, at least—another moral lesson: that all the hardships, even the most terrible ones, life puts in our way can be overcome. All it takes is a little daring, a sense of humor, and some ingenuity. Just look at Guido, who manages to save his small son, alone of all the other children in the camp, whose parents apparently didn't have the necessary daring, humor, and ingenuity. This lesson, too, is, of course, a positive and optimistic one—the good guys always win in the end!—readily acceptable and easy to embrace.

But as much as we'd like to believe in this maxim and let it warm our hearts, it still sounds hollow. Not only childish and simplistic in the context of the Holocaust, it also indirectly evokes the same mean spirit with which Israeli society used to reproach the survivors during the early years immediately after the Holocaust: "Why did you go like lambs to the slaughter?" "If only you'd stood and fought, instead of passively obeying and meekly accepting what the Germans did to you, things would have been different." This kind of attitude is not only an implied offense against the victims' memory and dignity—as if they can be held, even in theory, partly responsible for what the murderers did to them—but it reveals, yet again, a deep, cardinal misunderstanding of what happened in the Holocaust in general and in the concentration camps in particular.

The question "Why, out of all the Jews led to their deaths, a few somehow survived while the vast majority were indeed murdered?" troubled many people, including the survivors themselves. Primo Levi, for instance, expands on the subject in *The Drowned and the Saved.* As already mentioned, he writes that the prisoner's life in the camp "even apart from the hard labor, the beatings, the cold, and the illnesses" depended on his or her somehow obtaining additional nourishment to the deliberately inadequate food provided by the Germans, on which a person could survive for only two or three months—until "the physiological reserves of the organism were consumed," and the prisoner was doomed to "death by hunger, or by diseases induced by hunger." But getting the indispensable additional nourishment by whatever means necessary, "astute or violent, licit or illicit," wasn't solely dependent on the prisoner's own cleverness or ingenuity. As in everything else in the camps, in this, too, the prisoner was at the mercy of arbitrary chance.

Our natural human need for justice, or at least for some kind of order and reason, even in the cruel, absurd world of the Holocaust, makes us wish to believe that it wasn't mere chance that things went one way and not another. With no basis in fact, but only because we want so much to believe in some reasonable explanation, we tend to think that maybe the ones who survived were the more resourceful and perceptive, the quick-witted, those who knew which line to stand in, where it would be easier to steal food, and what kind of work was easier. Or maybe they were the immoral ones, those not above obtaining food "violently or illicitly"—or perhaps those who didn't give up and were determined to endure, those who rebelled, who didn't go "like lambs to the slaughter."

We only fool ourselves with these baseless rationalizations. In truth, all were murdered indiscriminately, those who obeyed and those who rebelled. Likewise, of those who collaborated with the Germans, some survived, but in many cases the collaborators were murdered, their collaboration notwithstanding. The same often happened to those who tried to hide or escape; to those who looked out only for themselves, who were informers or stole food from their friends; to the generous and goodhearted ones who selflessly helped others; to the strong and fit who could work; and to those who knew how to get by—and those who didn't. Sometimes people were actually saved because they were disabled or dwarves, since the camp doctor wanted to experiment on them; or because they were talented violinists, since the camp commander liked music and organized himself an orchestra from among the prisoners. But not all dwarves or violinists were saved; on the contrary, most were murdered. Just like most of the fit and strong, the informers, the cowards, and the generous ones, the immoral villains and the noble-hearted heroes.

The fact that those who stood in the right line yesterday were killed and those who stood in the left one were temporarily spared didn't mean that this was the way it was going to be today or tomorrow as well. You could stand in the "correct" line, but if one of the murderers didn't like something about you—you were too tall for his taste, or too short, or your nose or ears were too prominent, or too small—he'd order you to move to the other line or just shoot you on the spot. Or one day those who stood in the left line were killed while those who stood in the right one were spared. You could never foresee what would happen, and this uncertainty and disorientation were an integral, deliberate part of the torture the Nazis devised for their victims.

Moreover, the vast majority of those brought to the death camps didn't even have a chance to deal with the horrors of life as prisoners; they were murdered within hours. Only some of those deported from all over Europe were held in the camps as regular prisoners and forced laborers. The rules of life and death there did not follow any normal laws of logic. Life and death in the camps were for the most part a hell of arbitrating.

And that is the answer so difficult to accept. The victims' death or survival had very little to do, if it had anything to do at all, with the victims themselves. But Benigni, it seems at first glance, goes back to the same old, simplistic answers—as if the survival of a concentration camp prisoner was to a large measure in his own hands, and all he needed to do was to employ some humor and a little resourcefulness, to outwit the Germans and not go like a lamb to the slaughter. You could even save your little boy from the Nazis' clutches, the film seems to be telling us, with the help of three jokes, two tricks, and a little hocus-pocus.

But in effect, as the film itself abundantly demonstrates, what saves Giosue is not his father's tricks and wiles, but his own amazing talent for not being aware and not understanding what is going on around him. The almost unavoidable conclusion we must reach at the end of the film is that the child gets out of a concentration camp alive mostly because he's such an idiot.

It all begins for the child when he and his father are suddenly removed by force from their home and put on a truck together with the father's uncle, Eliseo, and other people as scared and as desperate as they are, with armed German guards watching them so they don't run away. The boy wants to know where they're going:

GIOSUE: Pop, come on, tell me where we're going.
GUIDO *(He hesitates, then improvises)*: We're . . . uh, we're going to . . . what's the name of that place? . . . You've asked me a thousand times, and I told you: I can't tell you!
GIOSUE: Uncle, where are we going? I'm so tired. . . .
UNCLE *(embarrassed)*: We're going. . . . *(But he doesn't know what to say.)*
GUIDO: Giosue, what do you mean, "Where are we going?" Come on, didn't you understand what I told you?
(Giosue shakes his head no.)
GUIDO: Okay, what's today? *(He smiles.)* Your birthday, right? You said you wanted to take a trip, didn't you? I've spent months planning this—come on, Giosue!
GIOSUE: Where are we going?
GUIDO: We're going . . . we're going. . . .
(He looks for an answer, but can't think of one. The child insists.)

GIOSUE: Where?
(*Guido, with a sly, conspiratorial look, lowers his voice.*)
GUIDO: No, I can't tell you. You know, I promised Mommy. If she finds out I told you she'll be angry at me. You know how she is. It's a surprise. It's—it makes me laugh. My daddy organized the same thing for me when I was little boy, will you laugh! Look, first we're going . . . when you get there, you'll see something and you'll say, "Oh!" but we won't be there long. Then a bell goes. . . .
GIOSUE: But where are we going?
(*Giosue smiles faintly, then yawns. A fast train goes by in front of the truck, and when it has passed, the truck starts on its way again.*)
GIOSUE: I'm tired.
GUIDO: Go on, sleep a little!
(*A second later, Guido stares into Uncle's eyes with a worried and disbeliev- ing expression.*)
GUIDO (*whispering*): Uncle, where are they taking us? Where are we going?
(*End of scene.*)

Do the two adults, Guido and Eliseo, know or understand where they're being taken and are just trying to hide it from the child in or- der to spare him the anguish? Or do they, like the child, not know or understand either? Apparently, the adults in this scene seem to know, or at least suspect, that they're going to their deaths, and they are hiding this terrible truth from the child.

In reality, of course, the Germans didn't inform those condemned to extermination of the fate awaiting them. Quite understandably, they went to great lengths in the opposite direction. In order to keep the victims in a state of constant fear, but always with a glimmer of hope for improvement of their lot—the most useful combination from the point of view of the Germans to ensure the fullest possible cooperation of the deportees and make the process of their deporta- tion easier—a vast, methodical system of deceit was employed. The Germans told the Jews that they were being sent to work camps, that they were being transferred east for "resettlement," and so on. As for the deportees, they indeed couldn't know or understand, particu- larly early on, where they were being sent. (As contemporary view- ers and readers, we must remind ourselves that the very notion of "extermination camp," both as a term and a concept, was a Nazi innovation. Contrary to its present prevalence, at that time the term didn't exist, not even as a possibility, in a normal person's

consciousness in Europe or anywhere else; only the Nazis themselves had a crystal-clear knowledge, all along, of what exactly the
designation meant.)

Later on, when rumors of the camps and of what went on in them
started to spread, despite the heavy screen of secrecy and the Germans' deception tactics, even the victims found them hard to believe. It was not only out of normal denial, a common psychological
defense mechanism people tend to subconsciously activate against
horror too great to grasp, especially horror against which they are
helpless whatever they do. Their disbelief was due also, quite simply, to the fact that any reasonable person found it very difficult to
get used to the thought that something like that was really happening, or could happen, in mid-twentieth-century Europe.

But when most deportees reached the camps, they didn't have
much trouble realizing, very quickly indeed, that the things taking
place there—as inhuman, absurd, and unprecedented as they
were—were really happening.

In the film, for the sake of his story, Benigni both has his cake and
eats it—Guido doesn't realize that the Germans are about to kill him
and his son, and he also protects his son from this very knowledge
that he supposedly doesn't have, in other words, that the Germans
are going to kill them.

But maybe Guido doesn't know for certain that the purpose of this
trip is death. By the way things are unfolding, maybe it's only apparent to him that this isn't a birthday trip, only that something really bad, even though unknown, is about to happen? Maybe that's
why he lies to his son—to defend him from the bad, unknown things
about to happen to them and the other people on the truck?

Yet all those ominous signs that the father sees and experiences
are simultaneously seen and experienced by Giosue as well. German
soldiers storm their house and forcefully remove them, without
even giving them the chance to pack a few things. The soldiers then
get them, along with others, on a truck whose destination is kept secret from its passengers. And all the adults taking part in this forced
trip—including his father and his uncle—are frightened, anxious,
and desperate.

The boy himself, unsurprisingly, is frightened and anxious, and
he asks his father, "Where are we going?" But neither the father
nor the uncle can answer him. They hesitate, stumble, and evade
his questions. Obviously the two adults' reactions should have

even further increased the child's anxiety and alarm. Instead, opt-ing to accept his father's ludicrous reply that it is all a surprise birthday trip his parents have arranged for him, he relaxes and falls asleep.

True, it's only a film, and this entire story, as some claimed (un-convincingly, in my opinion, as I explained in the previous chapter), is just a fairy tale, similar to when Red Riding Hood is capable of be-lieving that the wolf she sees in bed is really her grandmother. But in order to accept the idea that this sudden abduction from home and this grim trip in a truck are a birthday outing, in this situation, when the child has already seen German occupation soldiers march-ing through his town and heard from his father about the persecu-tion of Jews—he would have to have been not only stricken with a fabled naïveté even greater than that of Red Riding Hood but also blind and deaf, which we can well see he isn't.

And yet, a little further into the film, when the Jews are put on the train that will take them to the concentration camp, the father goes on playing the game, while the boy goes on playing the dupe.

> GUIDO: What time is it? Looks like we're leaving right on time! What organization! You've never been on a train, have you, Giosue?
> GIOSUE: No. What's it like? Is it nice?
> GUIDO: Fantastic. Inside there's all wood, no seats. Everybody stands.
> GIOSUE: No seats?
> GUIDO: Obviously you've never been. Are you kidding, seats on a train? Everybody stands, very close to everybody else. It's real fun.

Can't the child see what his father sees, what everyone there is able to see—that the soldiers are forcing the two of them and the others onto the train at gunpoint? Is he completely blind or termi-nally stupid? Or maybe he can't see anything because he's too short?

Indeed, how does the father know that these trains have no seats? Can he simply see that? And if so, why can't the child? Is that also because he's too short? Or does the father know that these trains have no seats because he has seen films on the Holocaust?

When Guido and Giosue arrive at the concentration camp, the film arrives at its core: in order to protect his son's life, so we are supposed to take it, the father makes up a sweet lie, telling the boy that all that is happening in the camp is just a game, and the prize for the winner—whoever first reaches 1,000 points—is a real tank.

Does the father already understand at this point that the Germans intend to kill all the prisoners through starvation, forced labor, or gas, and because of that realization he invents this game for his son? Or is the invention of the game only meant to make the hardships of camp life easier for his son to endure?

Later in the film, when the mother, Dora, is already in the camp, after having volunteered—out of love and devotion—to go there, an older woman prisoner named Gigliola (that's her name in the script; it isn't mentioned in the film itself) explains to her that the showers where the children and elderly inmates are taken are in fact gas chambers, where they're being killed.

As the film presents it, except for Gigliola, not a single one of the female inmates, including those being taken to their deaths, knows or realizes that going to the showers means death. Therefore, none of them cries or protests, not to mention resists. But how come, really, only Gigliola knows? Is this the first time a selection like this takes place? Probably not; otherwise, she herself could not know that those who go to the showers never return. How is it that only one of the women in the camp saw and heard and knew?

When you think about it, it's evident that this situation couldn't come about, neither in reality nor in the film, unless all the female prisoners were deliberately deaf and blind, and exceptionally stupid as well.

In the scene immediately following, Giosue sneaks into the foundry in which his father is a forced laborer. The father asks him, "Why aren't you with the other children?" and the boy, who never liked bathing, explains, "Because they said that today all the children have to take a shower, and I don't want to take a shower!" The father commands him, "Go right now and take that shower!" but the child refuses. And the father again commands, "Go take that shower!" Giosue persists in his refusal, and Guido gets angry: "You stubborn thing! I'm going to tell Mommy! You'll lose ten points!"

In other words, Guido, who's been in the camp for at least a few days or weeks, doesn't know that going to the showers means death. How come he hasn't seen, hasn't heard, and doesn't understand a thing? He's obviously as blind and as deaf as the rest, as well as stupendously stupid.

Yet just a scene later, the father suddenly orders his son, "From now on you have to hide all day!" Why? What did Guido suddenly see or realize that wasn't apparent earlier? His command makes it obvious that now he understands that the Germans are not only capable of killing all the prisoners, including him and his son, but also fully intend to do so. But what makes him realize this only now? How come he suddenly stops being stupid? Since the film doesn't provide any explanation to this radical change in Guido's perception of the situation, we can only guess that at this stage of the film, but not earlier, somebody finally let him read the script, and he duly discovered that the showers were gas chambers.

Later in the film, the father takes his son from his hiding place in the barrack—strangely disregarding the putative risk of exposing him in open daylight—and shows him German children, offspring of the camp's officers, to "prove" to him that the other prisoner children didn't go away, that is, died, but are only hiding like him, Giosue, because they're also participating in the game the father made up. As evidence, Guido sends Giosue to see who's hiding inside a small metal hut standing in the camp yard. The boy opens the small hut and is startled to see hidden inside it a boy described by his father as "blond," who is startled too and motions to Giosue to close the door, saying to him in German: "Sshh. Close the door, close it! I'm in here!" Giosue closes the door and returns to his father, happy as could be: "He's there, Pop! He's there!"

In other words, Giosue does not realize or even suspect, neither from his different look nor from his different clothes—maybe because his look and clothes aren't actually that different—that the boy in the hut isn't a prisoner child like him, but a German boy. Neither does Giosue notice that the boy doesn't speak Italian like the prisoners, but a language that even if he doesn't know enough to name it as German, he must know it to be the language of the camp's overlords. And so, since he manages to be deaf and blind, he doesn't find it very hard to be the complete dupe and swallow whole his father's fabrications.

After this, a German woman attendant takes Giosue in with the German children to dine in the camp officers' mess, without any of the Germans, neither the adults nor the children, noticing that Giosue isn't the child of a German officer but a camp prisoner; it seems that the Germans are just as blind and stupid as everyone else.

Thus, for the film's basic plot—the story about a father in a concentration camp who makes up a game to save his son's life—to be possible, all of the participants—the father, the child, the mother, the uncle, all of the prisoners, and all of the jailers—must simultaneously be blind, deaf, and stupid.

The film, as we have seen, plays a two-way game: on the one hand, it lets the viewers understand that the father invents the game to protect his child and save his life; on the other hand, it portrays the father as not understanding himself, at least up to a certain, quite late, point, what is really happening in the camp. But if Guido truly doesn't realize that the real game is murder, why does he have to make up the false, sugar-coating game? What is he really trying to shield his son from?

The assumption the father makes when inventing the game—and the film goes along with him—is that the most important, the crucial thing for the good of the child in this situation is to hide the truth from him.

The great danger from which the father protects his child is not death at the hands of the Germans, but seeing reality as it is. Otherwise he would probably tell him: "Do you see what's going on here, Giosue? These soldiers here, the Germans, the Nazis, they want to kill us—me, you, Bartholomew, Uncle Eliseo, everyone in here. This isn't a game. This is for real. They really want to kill us. That's why we can't let them get you, and you have to hide all the time."

If the father's purpose is to protect his son's life, then the story he tells him, and the story that the film tells us, is based on the assumption that a six-year-old child isn't intelligent or mature enough to understand mortal fear and act accordingly; hence, in order to make him behave the way we want him to, we must feed him an infantile fable fit for his limited understanding.

But anyone who is even slightly familiar with children can see that a six-year-old, any six-year-old, is sensible enough to easily grasp mortal danger—especially in this specific situation of a camp that is supposed to be crawling with armed, omnipotent murderers, eliminating first, no questions asked, any child they come across. Any six-year-old wants to live and will do anything to escape death. Small, weak, and still very much dependent on the adults surrounding him, he may make errors of judgment, but he is plainly capable of cooperating with them in a struggle for survival.

What is your best course of action if you wish to save your child in a situation like Guido's in the concentration camp? Tell him he has to hide because the Germans might kill him—or that he has to hide because it will win him a real tank, or a trip to Disneyland, or whatever? Which of these strategies has the greater chance of making the child hide and behave exactly as told?During the Holocaust, six-year-old children became quite grown up overnight. They didn't usually need much explanation to grasp what was happening around them. Many of the accounts by people who survived that time as children prove that they completely understood how great the danger was and so had no difficulty behaving accordingly.

As an example, I would like to present a short segment of an interview with Holocaust survivor Itamar Orian, who was born Jerzy (Jurek) Trybel and, as a child, was imprisoned in the Warsaw ghetto along with his mother, grandfather, and grandmother.

From Orian's videotaped testimony:

ORIAN: And then the actions started [the word "action" here refers to the German term "Aktion," used by the Nazis to designate the operation of evacuating and deporting the Jews from the ghettos to the extermination camps.—K.N.]. "Actions"—that means they start taking people away, we didn't know where back then, but we felt, all of us, it wasn't good at all . . . and at that time, those who worked somewhere, and could prove they had a job—were supposedly safe from evacuation. Then they worked in what was called "workshops"; and Mother worked in one of those, but I stayed home. And then we found out that when people went out to work, they [the Germans] came and took out those who remained home.

So then people started making "bunkers" [hideouts]. And they made me a "bunker," first it was inside a pile of newspapers which we had in the room; I mean they made this "hideyhole" inside of this pile, and I'd get in there, they'd put me inside in the morning, and they'd take me out in the evening. That was at first. Then we realized it wasn't so good, because I still needed to relieve myself while I was in there, so we put this potty in, and you could sense [smell] this potty. So they made me this "bunker" under the coal in the kitchen. They put planks of wood in the corner between the floor and the wall, then put me in, and put coal on top. And once when I was sitting there, they must've taken out Grandpa and Grandma.

INTERVIEWER: Did you hear anything?

ORIAN: Yes, of course I heard.

INTERVIEWER: What did you hear?

ORIAN: "Hande hoch! Raus, raus, du varflucht Jude!" ["Hands up! Out, out, accursed Jew!"] And I was probably saved because the German soldiers relieved themselves on that coal. Some urinated, one defecated. It was all right, I stayed, a little wet, under the coal, but I stayed alive.

INTERVIEWER: You're telling here a very hard story for a child that age—sitting for a whole day from sunrise until Mom returns from work, inside this little hole. It must have been like eternity, to sit like that for a whole day.

ORIAN: I think it was, for Ghetto children, normal. There wasn't anything special about it. You knew that either you sit—or you're gone. It was a kind of very serious game. And children know how to play games. But it was obvious that it was a game for real. And that if you lose—you lose, you don't have to sit anywhere ever again, you're done for. Back then that somehow seemed normal to a child. It was very, very normal. That thing, that they pissed and shitted on me, that I remember to this day, and I—won't forget, won't forget, and won't forgive them, I won't forget this. But as to your question, for Ghetto children, it's mostly irrelevant. I mean—it was normal. We were very grown up, I'd say.

INTERVIEWER: Did you know it wasn't a game?

ORIAN: Yes, sure. I knew it was a game against death. But death wasn't so frightening.

INTERVIEWER: Why?

ORIAN: Because it happened to everybody.

INTERVIEWER: How old were you back then?

ORIAN: It was in '42. I was six.[1]

In other words—returning to the film—had the father really wanted to protect his six-year-old child, he should perhaps impress on him the gravity of the situation instead of hiding it from him. Furthermore, it's reasonable to assume that, by denying Giosue the knowledge that he is in mortal danger, Guido not only does not protect his son's life but actually increases the danger the child is in.

A possible conclusion: more than the father wishes to protect his son from impending murder, he wants to prevent him from understanding that he, like all the camp's prisoners, is going to be murdered sooner or later. The game's aim is not to defend the child and save his life, but to prevent him at all costs from realizing what is really happening. The great danger here isn't the murder, but knowing the truth about it.

The crux of the matter is that this entire story, in which the child believes his father's outlandish fabrication, couldn't have happened unless the child himself was blind, deaf, and stupid. Hence the script attempts time and again to convince the viewers that he is.

And indeed, there are at least two scenes in the film that prove that the scriptwriters did feel some doubt at a certain point, questioning whether the boy could really be 100 percent deaf and blind, as well as such a fool. In these scenes, he is allowed to behave as though he can hear, see, and understand the truth, and even try to confront it with his father's fabrication.

The first is the following exchange between the father and the child:

GUIDO: . . .So, did you play with the other kids today?
GIOSUE: Yes, but they don't know any of the rules. They said it's not true that you win a tank. They don't know about the points and scores.
(Guido takes a piece of bread from his pocket.)
GUIDO: They know, they know. They're just being tricky, don't fall for it. Everyone wants that tank. What, no tank? Are we kidding here?

And the child is convinced, because his father seemingly talks sense, and besides, any sensible child would choose to believe his beloved father and not some unknown children, even if the facts seem to agree with them and not with the father.

In the second scene, the boy protests to his father:

GIOSUE: They make buttons and soap out of us.
GUIDO: Giosue, what are you talking about?
GIOSUE: They cook us in the ovens.
GUIDO: Who told you that?
GIOSUE: A man was crying and he said they make buttons and soap out of us.
(Guido bursts out laughing.)
GUIDO: Giosue! You fell for it again! And here I thought you were a sharp kid! *(He smiles.)* Buttons and soap. Right. And tomorrow morning I'm washing my hands with Bartholomew and buttoning my jacket with Francesco and my vest with Claudio. . . .
(He is laughing as he pulls a button off his jacket and lets it fall to the floor.)
GUIDO: Uh-oh, Giorgio fell off!
(He picks up the button and puts it in his pocket.)
GUIDO: They make buttons out of people? What else?
GIOSUE: They cook us in ovens!
GUIDO: They cook us in ovens? I've heard of a wood-burning oven, but I never heard of a people-burning oven. Oh, I'm out of wood, pass me that lawyer over there! No, that lawyer's no good, he's not dry!

Come on, Giosue, get with it! Let's get serious now. Tomorrow morning there's a sack race with the bad guys, and you. . . .

In other words, the child now sees and understands the truth, or
at least something very similar to the truth in its horror and absurdity. (It's hard to tell, based on the film, whether Roberto Benigni
knows that the "soap made out of Jews" story was just a dread ru-
mor spread toward the end of the war but later found by historians
who studied the subject to be false. The corpses of Auschwitz victims were used as various industrial raw materials—their shaved
hair, for instance, was used for making blankets, mattresses, and
ropes; and their gold teeth were melted for reuse—but they were not
used for manufacturing soap.) But the father still keeps lying to his
son, even after the boy has understood that monstrous atrocities are
being committed around them, and the two of them, just like all the
other prisoners, are meant to become, sooner or later, victims as
well.

But why? Why does the father choose to keep up this false game,
when it becomes clear to him that his son understands the truth?

You would expect the father to have told him, now that he finds
out, if he didn't know it earlier, that his son is a smart little boy who
sees and understands what's going on—"That's true, kiddo, you're
right. I tried to hide it from you, so you won't get scared. But now
that you've found out for yourself they're going to kill all of us, me
and you, too, I want you to hide and do everything I tell you to,
understand?"—and the child would understand. Because he's actually already understood.

But Guido persists, even now, in clinging to his false story with
seemingly irrational stubbornness. Why? There are two possible reasons, which are actually not contradictory but complementary: (1) if
Guido doesn't cling to the tank-reward story and doesn't convince his
son to cling to it, the film will be impossible to end with a scene of the
child leaving his hiding place and coming face to face with an American tank, which will "prove" to him that his father's tall tale was indeed true; and (2), again, the father's chief aim is not really to save his
son's life. The really important thing for him is to prevent his son—
that is, the next generation—from knowing the truth about what is
happening in the concentration camp, in other words, about what
happened in the Holocaust.

But despite his father's "amusing" explanations in this scene, the boy refuses this time to go on believing in the false game, and he interrupts his father's attempts at convincing him: "No, Pop, that's enough, I want to go home." And the scene continues:

GUIDO: Now?
GIOSUE: Right now.
GUIDO: It's raining now. You'll come down with a terrible fever!
GIOSUE: I don't care. Let's go.
GUIDO: Okay, you want to go home, we'll go!
(He gets onto the bed and folds the blanket.)
GIOSUE *(amazed)*: Can we really go?
GUIDO: Sure! You don't think they force people to stay here, do you? *(He thinks a minute.)* We drop out, they cancel us. Too bad. We were winning, too.
(He pretends to look for a suitcase.)
GUIDO: Some other kid's going to win the real tank.
GIOSUE: Which kid? There aren't any more kids, I'm the only one left.
(Guido jumps down from the bed.)
GUIDO: No more kids? It's full of kids, it's busting with kids.
GIOSUE: Yeah? Where are they?
GUIDO: Hiding. They're not allowed to come out. It's full of kids hiding. It's a serious game.
GIOSUE: I don't get this game. How many points do we have?
(Guido opens the barracks door. It is pouring outside.)
GUIDO: Six hundred eighty-seven. I've told you a thousand times, we're first. We're winning! But never mind, we'll drop out. Let's go! I saw the chart yesterday. We'll go anyway, though. 'Bye, Bartholomew. Giosue and I are leaving. We're fed up here.
GUIDO *(to Bartholomew)*: The tank is done, it's ready. Clean the spark plugs off before you start it. Open the throttle. Otherwise the cannon will get stuck with the trucks. And the gun, did you see how nice it is? It came out beautiful! Lift the emergency brake before you move! Giosue and I are going. Giosue wants to quit. We could have gone back with the tank soon, but we'll take the bus today. So long, everybody. We're tired of this place. Let's go, or we'll miss the bus.
GIOSUE: It's raining, I'll come down with a terrible fever!
(And he starts to move toward the door. He looks at the rain. Giosue is standing still, confused.)

And then Giosue suddenly decides to believe his father and stay. The boy who was, for a moment, intelligent and perceptive goes back to being an idiot. Falsehood defeats truth. So the script demands.

From this point on to the end of the film, the child raises no further doubts and accepts his father's false story without protest. And, at the end of the film, he indeed "wins" a real tank as promised, the tank leading the American army column that captures the camp and frees its prisoners.

Do the viewers discover now, at the film's ending, that the boy actually knew and understood all along what the real game was, and just pretended—out of precocious wisdom and maturity, and to allay his father's fears—to be duped by the false game story? No.

Or perhaps now, after it's all over, the boy finally understands that the story his father made up wasn't true, and its only purpose was to protect him? No again.

Even now—after his father died, after he has been freed from the concentration camp, after it all ended—the boy continues to not understand a thing. And when he meets his mother at the end of the film he tells her, "We won!" and explains: "A thousand points! Couldn't you just die laughing? We came in first! We get to take the tank home! We won!"

Who won?

The father's make-believe sham, according to which everything that took place in the Holocaust was nothing but a game, won over the truth. In the face of all that he experienced, saw, heard, and perceived, the boy remained blind, deaf, and stupid; even in hindsight, he hasn't understood or learned anything.

And that's another moral, not any less important than the other moral lessons that the film teaches us, although this one is taught only implicitly, by example: to survive, to live, you have to lie, you must live a lie. And to live like that, in a lie, you have to be deliberately deaf and blind. In fact, it's highly advisable to pretend to be a complete idiot as well.

Exactly the same game that Guido offered to the six-year-old Giosue is that which Benigni offers to the viewers of *Life Is Beautiful*. Just as Guido used every trick, made every effort, to hide from his son the truth of the concentration camp where they were imprisoned, that is, the truth of the Holocaust, so the film does to its viewers: it hides from them, through tricks and deception, the truth of the Holocaust. And indeed, the film seems to provide us with proof that falsity can win. All that it takes is that people willingly close their eyes, seal their ears, refuse to understand—and then, evidently, it is quite possible to see no evil, hear no evil. In this sense, the film actually identifies with those tens of millions of European Christians who did exactly as it suggests: those who were, or pretended to be, blind, deaf, and completely ignorant in the face of the extermination of the Jews.

In the film, the young boy has no choice but to refuse to see the truth, to act as if he is willingly deaf and blind, and to generally behave like a dupe—since the scriptwriters wrote him that way. But why do most of the film's viewers behave exactly like the onscreen child? Who cast them in the role of dupes?

NOTES

1. USHMM Record Group 50, "Oral History, Israel Documentation Project, Interview with Itamar Orian," interviewer: Nathan Beyrak, project director of the joint project of the Fortunoff Video Archive for Holocaust Testimonies at Yale University and the United States Holocaust Memorial Museum. The United States Holocaust Memorial Museum gratefully acknowledges Jeff and Toby Herr for making this interview possible.

Chapter 4

A World without Jews

Viewers find out only halfway through the film that the hero, Guido, is a Jew. This transpires when harassing thugs paint on his uncle's horse the words "Attention, Jewish horse!" The uncle must presumably be a Jew then, and in that case we may deduce that, like his uncle, Guido is Jewish as well. The uncle even warns him in this scene, "You'll have to get used to it, Guido. They [the anti-Semites] will start on you, too"—which is absolute news for Guido as well as for the viewers. There's a distinct impression here that up to this moment, he never as much as suspected that he was "one of those."

Up to this point, for almost an hour of the film, it was never directly stated or even somehow implied that the protagonist was Jewish. Indeed, throughout the entire film and the script on which it was based, Guido does not have a single Jewish attribute, not even one tiny characteristic to reflect his supposed origins or ethnic, religious, or community affiliation. Not in his language—for instance, not even a word or two in Hebrew, Yiddish, Ladino, or Ghettaiolo ("Ghetto Speech," a mix of Italian and Hebrew, in which Italian Jews sometimes addressed each other)—some remnants of an everyday ritual blessing or a shred of a prayer; not in his appearance—perhaps a yarmulke or a beard and sidelocks, a fringed garment, or some other traditional clothing; and not in his customs—a mezuzah on his door, a ritual circumcision for his son, lighting Shabbat or Hanukah candles, shunning pork or lobster, fasting on Yom Kippur, a Passover Seder in his home, not even the exchange of some common greeting between him and his uncle or fellow Jews. Not "Shalom," not "Shabbat Shalom," not "Hag Sameach" (happy holiday), not "Mazal Tov" (congratulations), not "Shema Israel" ("Hear, O Israel"), not any traditionally Jewish association. None.

The Jew in this film has nothing Jewish about him.

The only thing, therefore, which is perhaps supposed to identify him as a Jew is his physical appearance: a not particularly handsome individual, boasting a not particularly short nose. It's pure coincidence that that's just how Roberto Benigni, the non-Jewish actor who plays him, looks like; but just as coincidentally, this is also, of course, the automatic visual stereotype of the "Jew" in European popular culture in general and in Christian anti-Semitic popular culture in particular.

But apart from that, does Guido, as a character, have a "Jewish" personality or certain "Jewish" attributes—if such attributes indeed exist—and if so, what are they?

On careful examination, several attributes can be identified in Guido's character and behavior, and they are, in no particular order, as follows: he is a simple man, unschooled and unskilled, yet he dreams of opening a bookshop and goes on to realize his dream; hence he is a book lover; he is an amusing person, a graceful and charming jester, or at least the film attempts to portray him as such; he scorns convention and rebels against it; he is physically weak and clumsy, inept as a handyman; he's exceedingly childish, as egocentric as a baby, as reckless as a little boy; he is compulsive in general, and particularly so as a lover, a tendency that the film portrays as romantic; he is a liar and a thief, an impersonator and a charlatan; he's an exploiter—his whole relationship with his friend Ferruccio, for example, is an ongoing, one-sided exploitation; he is sharp and witty but, on the other hand, in many episodes in the film, he acts like a complete idiot; he is a warm family man—a loving and devoted husband, a wonderful father; and he's a dreamer and a schemer, with an almost infinite imagination and unending resourcefulness.

Aside from the explicit information the film provides us with at a relatively late stage regarding his ethnic background, and apart from our direct impression of his physical appearance, these are Guido's distinguishing attributes as a plot character. Which of these can be seen as the personality traits of a Jew or as typical "Jewish" characteristics? And why, in a more general way, was Guido's character constructed the way it was? Why did Benigni, Guido's creator, choose to endow him with these particular attributes and not with others?

To a considerable extent, Guido's attributes were predetermined, since they are the stock characteristics required by the genre to which the film belongs, that is, by the fact that *Life Is Beautiful* is a more or less classic romantic comedy.

The rules and formulas of romantic comedy as a genre, as they largely evolved in the Hollywood of the 1930s, still remain almost unchanged. Generally, the term defines a comedy telling the story of a pair of lovers whose love is thwarted for one reason or another, and so they struggle in various—and, of course, funny—ways against all kinds of obstacles and opponents standing in their way until they finally prevail, and the film concludes with a happy ending, in other words, the lovers are united, get married, and become a happy family.

The subgenre of "social" or "class" romantic comedy, to which *Life Is Beautiful* specifically belongs, has deep historical roots in the European popular theater. (In its Israeli version, it is known as "a *burekas* film"—*burekas* being cheap, ethnic, popular street food.) In this subgenre, a member of the lower class or an ethnic group considered inferior in the society in which the plot is set falls in love with a member of a higher class or someone from an ethnic background considered superior, to the great resentment and consternation of the beloved's family; the "inferior" lover then stubbornly courts his or her "unsuitable" love object to the happy end.

The unwanted suitor—let's keep to the male pronoun, as it is the one relevant here—ultimately achieves his goal and marries his high-class sweetheart. Afterwards, toward the end of the film, the resentful, disdainful "superior" family realizes that he is actually a charming person, a devoted husband, and an exemplary father who makes their daughter very happy and provides them with wonderful grandchildren. And so their hearts melt, they accept the marriage, they are reconciled with their lower-class in-law and his "inferior" relatives, and they all become one big happy family.

And indeed, many of Guido's attributes are part and parcel of his being the suitor in a romantic "class" comedy: in order to conform to the conventions of the subgenre, he must be a simple man, with no schooling or social standing; his courting behavior must be compulsive, or, if you will, exceedingly romantic; he sometimes has no choice, because of the subgenre's basic plot requirements, but to lie and impersonate in order to reach his goal; he is always—and that's also a part of the subgenre—more cunning and clever than his higher-class opponents; on the other hand, sometimes, because of his social limitations, he acts like a complete idiot; of course, like in any such film, he disregards accepted norms and conventions, which is apparent in the very fact of his courting someone out of his social class; eventually, inevitably, by the rules of the subgenre, after the woman accepts him and they have a family, he must become a devoted husband and exemplary father—to the great surprise, but also joy, of her resentful family; and he must obviously be amusing and charming, or else this wouldn't be a romantic comedy, the film wouldn't be funny, and the noble-born woman wouldn't have fallen for him.

Some of Guido's personality traits probably owe to the fact that scriptwriter Benigni knew in advance that he would play Guido and therefore gave his character attributes that he plays well, namely, he made him a clown. Indeed, a number of Guido's characteristics come directly from the classic clown archetype: his being weak and clumsy and not good with his hands; his characteristic clownish compulsiveness, as well as his propensity for impersonation; his childishness, egocentrism, and recklessness, which are fundamental elements of the clown's persona; the traditional association with the clown as a dreamer with a great imagination; and the fact that every clown, of course, is amusing and full of charm.

A romantic comedy of the ethnic-class subgenre will also predictably use some additional stock attributes that are supposed to represent the protagonist's particular ethnic background—Black, Chinese, Moroccan, Romanian, Hispanic, Polish, Yemenite, and so forth. Guido in *Life Is Beautiful* is, therefore, not only a lower-class, simple-hearted lover, as the genre demands, and not only a typical clown to enable him to serve as a suitable showcase for his creator's particular talents, but he is also supposed to be a "representative Jew." But how is that evident? Which attributes did Benigni give him that belong neither to the unaristocratic lover nor to the classic clown to make him implicitly or explicitly identifiable as a member of a specific ethnic group?

To his long-nosed, unhandsome looks—which are, again, an inevitable physical attribute that actor Benigni brings to Guido's imaginary character, thus necessarily making it an integral part of the Jewish protagonist that scriptwriter Benigni created—we can, at this point, add the three attributes left to Guido after accounting for those pertinent to his lower-class romantic and clown aspects. These are thief, exploiter, and book lover. All of them, incidentally or otherwise, are the familiar attributes associated for centuries with Jews and not always by devout philo-Semites.

Hence, Guido's character in *Life Is Beautiful* looks and acts, for some reason, as an incarnation of "the thieving, exploitative, book-loving, ugly, long-nosed Jew" of popular anti-Semitic stigma.

One thing, anyway, is beyond doubt: Benigni did not create a Jewish character as a Jew might subjectively view himself "from the inside"; and indeed, Guido doesn't for a moment perceive himself as a Jew.

When Giosue, Guido's six-year-old son, reads the sign forbidding the entry of dogs and Jews into a shop in their hometown, he doesn't ask his father, "Why aren't we or dogs allowed in the shop, Daddy?" but "Why aren't Jews or dogs allowed in the shop, Daddy?" That is, it doesn't occur to the child to think of himself as a Jew. And this, we are led to assume, is because his father, as he was created in the script and onscreen, never taught him what it is exactly that makes him a Jew; he probably never even told him that they were Jewish at all.

And in this he is quite consistent. In the scene where Guido goes to the municipality to ask for a permit for opening his bookshop, he suddenly remembers, as he sits down, that the eggs he received from a village girl in an earlier scene are still in his pocket, and says: "Madonna, the eggs. We nearly had a real omelette here." (This appears in the Italian original; in the English translation, he says "Oh, Lord, the eggs," while in Hebrew he says, "Oh God, the eggs." These variations in the different languages are not insignificant.) A little later, when he drops a flowerpot on Inspector Rodolfo's head, he looks down the window to see what happened and says: "Madonna, what a hit!" (in English: "Jesus, what a hit!" and in Hebrew: "What a hit!") Later still, when he is courting Dora, he looks for a key for her heart, as it were, and tells her: "Maybe the Madonna will throw it down," and then, to trick Dora into thinking that the Virgin Mary indeed complies with and performs small amusing miracles for him, he turns to the sky and shouts: "Maria! The key!" (He knows from an earlier scene that doing so makes a woman appear in the upper-floor window and throw down a key.)

Granted, in all these cases it is clear that the presumably Jewish Guido evokes St. Mary's name not because he believes in her but as a mere common figure of speech, just like any of the Christian Italians among whom he lives would speak, in an offhand way, not necessarily related to the name's original, religious significance; just as easily as an American Jew, or for that matter an Israeli one, would say "Jesus Christ!" with no intention of converting to Christianity or giving up his or her Jewish self-definition. But this example does provide one additional small proof that Guido, who is supposed to be Jewish, isn't different in any way from the non-Jews in the film.

But why shouldn't we view Guido as just another secular Jew, completely assimilated into his surrounding society and lacking any regard or connection to his origins or to Judaism in general? That too is a legitimate, albeit latent, way of being Jewish. Jewish religious law itself, the Halakhah, at least since the times of the Second Temple, defines a person as indisputably Jewish by the mere fact of being born to a Jewish mother; no further proof or distinguishing trait is required. This holds true even if the person in question does not live as a Jew, does not show any commitment to Judaism, and never does a single thing that would identify him or her as a member of the Jewish people or religion.

No comparison is intended, of course, but the Nazis also had a keen interest in defining precisely "who is a Jew." According to their Racial Laws[1] and the complex bureaucratic directives accompanying them, a person was considered a "complete" Jew—again, independent of the person's behavior or his or her own self definition—if born to three Jewish grandparents; those who had only two "full" Jewish grandparents were considered as "half Jewish," or *Mischlige*; but should such a "half Jew" have joined a Jewish community or married a Jew, he or she would automatically become a "full" Jew by law. In addition, those born after a certain date of mixed marriages, or of sexual relations between a Jew and a non-Jew outside of marriage, were also considered "full" Jews.

In Guido's case, it's impossible to tell whether he is a kind of "latent Jew" according to the Jewish religious definition or just according to the Nazi Racial Laws, which have, in fact, more relevance in his case than Jewish religious definitions in light of what happens to him as a Jew. We only know that he doesn't see himself as Jewish in any way.

There were, of course, many assimilated, secular Jews in Europe at the time in question, and a great many of them were persecuted, tortured, and murdered for their Jewishness—even though they were alienated from it out of deliberate choice or simple loss of interest, and never saw it as part of their identity or self-definition. So from this perspective, it was wholly conceivable to meet in Italy in the 1940s such a non-Jewish Jew—a kind of Jewish gentile, whose non-Jewishness does nothing at all to stop the Nazis from sending him to a concentration camp.

But two things here beg further inquiry, in the film's context. One is the fact that Benigni chose precisely this kind of Jew and no other—in other words, one lacking any specific "Jewish" trait—as the protagonist of his film. The other is the fact that not only Guido but also all of the Jews in the film are, without a single exception, such non-Jewish Jews.

Uncle Eliseo is supposed to be Jewish like Guido. But what is Jewish about him? Just like with Guido—nothing. Perhaps Eliseo, like his nephew, is completely assimilated. Could be. But even assimilated families in Italy often maintained a few Jewish traditions and attributes. Dan Vittorio Segre, who was the same age as the real Primo Levi and the fictional Guido Orefice of *Life Is Beautiful*, was born to an assimilated family and even became—without hiding his Jewishness—a member of the Fascist youth movement. In his book, *Memoirs of a Fortunate Jew*,[2] he writes:

> My father used to recite by heart, morning and evening, a small section of the Shema, the Biblical passage that forms the center of the daily liturgy. He also carried in his wallet the text of the Kaddish, a sanctification of God also recited by mourners, printed in Latin characters on a card. . . . I had to go Thursdays afternoon to the lesson at the Talmud Torah to prepare for my Bar Mitzvah. . . . At Passover, we ate matzoh.

And he goes on to evoke several further customs preserved in his family.

Primo Levi, in *Is This a Man?* (*Survival in Auschwitz*), tells how some of the Italian Jewish inmates behaved when they found out that they were being deported to an unknown destination:

> All took leave from life in the manner which most suited them. Some praying. . . . They [the pious women] unloosened their hair, took off their shoes, placed the Yahrzeit [annual remembrance of the dead] candles on the ground and lit them according to the customs of their fathers, and set on the bare soil in a circle for the lamentations, praying and weeping all the night.

But it's not only these two Jews, Eliseo and Guido, whom we meet in the pre-Holocaust first half of the film, who lack a single Jewish trait. None of the hundreds of Jews in the second half of the film, taking place in the Holocaust, has any Jewish attribute either, not even an implied one. This is true for the Jews being taken to the concentration camp in the truck and on the train, as well as for the Jews who arrive at the camp and are imprisoned in it—in Guido's barrack, during forced labor in the foundry, and in the women's camp where Dora is held. Not one of them even bears a Jewish name.

Those who have names in the script and film are called Bartholomew, Gigliola, Vittorio, Alfonso, Giorgio, Claudio, and Francesco. All common, neutral Italian names, some with clear Christian connotations. Bartholomew, of course, was one of the twelve apostles. St. Francesco of Assisi founded the Franciscan order, which at a later stage turned into a backbone of the Catholic Inquisition that waged zealous war against the Jewish faith and persecuted the Marranos, Spanish Jews who tried to pass as Christians.

Thus every one of the Jews in this film, without exception, could be easily considered as Christians for all intents and purposes. Not in the religious sense, of course—there are no crucifixes hanging from their necks, they don't pray to the Holy Trinity, and they don't participate in any religious ritual—but in the sense that they are no different in any way from all the Christian Italians among whom they live who don't wear crucifixes or take part in any Christian worship either.

It's quite possible, of course, that Benigni doesn't know Jews and never met any, and the difference between them and other people, if it exists, isn't clear to him and anyway doesn't really interest him, and that's why all the Jews he created turned out similar to their Christian neighbors. On the other hand, it may not be too much to expect of a filmmaker, who intends to make a film about a certain group of people to which he himself does not belong—and whose ethnic or cultural identity is a major topic in his film, albeit in a negative way (they are being persecuted because of it)—to do some rudimentary research and to learn something of the customs of these people, their traditional clothing, their language, their rituals, and their general lifestyle, so that he can, if he wishes to, characterize his protagonists in an authentic way.

It's impossible to tell from either the film or the script whether Benigni knows any Jews of whatever kind or made any research about them. But it's obvious that by deliberately choosing not to characterize his protagonists as "Jews" in any acceptable, recognizable manner, Benigni actually obliterated the Jewishness of his film's Jews.

Can we dismiss this choice, too, as legitimate for the film's purpose or perhaps as some insignificant glitch, like some kind of script typo or camera malfunction?

Let's suppose the film were telling a story about the arrest of an uncle and his nephew, both black, the nephew's white wife, and their small child in a South African detention camp for black political prisoners during the Apartheid regime. And let's suppose that the nephew and the uncle, who, we are told, are black, and the child, whom you'd naturally expect to be black at least to a degree, as well as all the other detainees in the black people's detention camp, were all, to the last one, played by a white cast. Could we, in that case, dismiss the scriptwriter-director's choice as meaningless? Would we not feel then, as viewers, that something was plainly out of joint— and by no means accidentally, but in the most calculated way—in the film we are being shown?

Choosing white people to play the roles of blacks would no doubt be perceived as extremely meaningful. We could surely assume that the film's creator consciously employed an antiracist mechanism of artificial "alienation" to demonstrate to his white viewers what it's like to be persecuted and repressed and to mock their prejudices by showing them that "blacks are humans just like us." But then we could still ask him or her: "To whom, in your opinion, do you need to prove such an elementary truth? Who is the target audience to which you're trying to convey your message?" In other words: what does "They are humans just like us" mean? Who are "they," and who are "us"?

Did Roberto Benigni also decide to prove that "the Jews aren't any different from us; look, they're human beings too" (meaning, similar to Benigni's own group, the European Christians)? Did he assume that were his film's protagonists to look or behave too "Jewish," it would make it difficult for his audience to identify with them? Is that the reason he opted for making it as easy as possible for any viewer— that is, any non-Jewish viewer—to realize that "Jews don't have horns or tails; they're actually ordinary people just like you and me"?

This hypothesis would explain why Guido's Jewishness remains hidden for the entire first hour of the film. The prolonged exposition of the protagonist as a "regular" person with a "neutral" ethnic, cultural, and religious identity thus enables the viewers, at least Christian viewers, to fully identify with the main character before he begins to suffer exclusion and persecution for being a Jew. The same way that casting white people in black people's roles would imply a basic assumption that the suffering of blacks would insufficiently move potential (white) viewers, so there may in this case be at play an implied assumption—or a prejudice—that the suffering of a Jew isn't moving enough, doesn't bring about automatic empathy.

By the way, it's worth noting that, incidentally or otherwise, the protagonists of the two most successful previous Oscar-winning Holocaust films weren't Jewish. In Steven Spielberg's *Schindler's List*, the hero is a Catholic ethnic German, who saves hundreds of Jews from death in Auschwitz. In *Sophie's Choice*,[3] the protagonist is a Catholic Polish woman imprisoned in Auschwitz during the war, where she is forced, according to the story, to choose which one of her children will die and which will go on living. The hundreds of thousands of real Jewish mothers, who were not given even this much of a choice, somehow never stimulated the imaginations of filmmakers and the general public enough for their personal stories to make it into popular films. They remained anonymous, shadowy figures, part of that great obscure crowd of "those Jews who disappeared in the camps."

Returning to *Life Is Beautiful*, in obliterating any Jewish trait in his characters, Benigni seems to be saying that what the Germans did to the Jews was wrong—because "the Jews are ordinary people just like you and me."

Wonderful. But what if the Jews—in the film or indeed in life— were actually some foreign creatures? Consider the males sporting beards and sidelocks, the females covering their shaved heads with elaborate wigs and scarves; people who speak Yiddish or Ladino, wear strange clothes, take part in some obscure religious rituals, deny the godliness of Christ, and maybe even lend money with interest and smell of garlic. Would it then be all right to discriminate against them, to persecute them, to exterminate them in gas chambers?

Racism begins with not accepting the other as an equal and may lead to Auschwitz. The way from the one to the other is perhaps a long one, but it is definitely straight and consistent. To really believe in equality means to accept the other as totally equal to oneself in his or her rights and basic humanity, even if that person is totally different in appearance or customs. Hence when you claim—directly or implicitly—that you are willing to accept the other as equal, but only on the condition that he or she concede and disown what makes him or her distinct, so that the other becomes exactly like you—you are taking, by implication, a first, small, but significant step toward sliding down a very slippery and dangerous slope.

The Germans physically destroyed the Jews by isolating and starving them in ghettos and by systematically killing them by the millions with the aim of annihilating them and realizing their ideological dream—a world without Jews. Roberto Benigni, of course, just made a film—a romantic comedy that touched the hearts of tens of millions. He didn't harm anybody; all he did in his film was to "take the Jewishness out of the Jew" and with that obliterate the Jew's identity. Needless to say, there is all the difference in the world—practical, ideological, moral, legal, human—between his act and those of active and self-proclaimed Jew-haters.

In his approach to the Jews, as it is expressed in this film, there is one troubling point, however, that could be understood as another form of annihilation, not a physical, but a spiritual one. Were Benigni's approach universally implemented, were the Jews to be made to lose any trace of Jewishness, the result would be somewhat similar—even if reached by wholly different means, utterly humane and completely friendly. We'd all stay alive, but in a world without Jews.

The Nazis persecuted and exterminated the groups they deemed "undesirable"—Jews, Gypsies, the sick and disabled, people politically on the left (communists and social democrats), homosexuals—just for being what they were. The victims, too, knew what they were being persecuted for. The Jews, who were the main and consistent target of the persecution and extermination policy, knew they were being persecuted and exterminated for being what they were. The persecution and extermination had not only an end, but a cause as well.

Benigni's film conceals and obscures not only the mass systematic murder and the identity of the victims, but also the very reason for the Holocaust. The film doesn't make it clear, not to the child Giosue who is taken there or to the viewers, why these specific people were gathered from all over Italy, maybe Europe, and put in the concentration camp.

The reason why Guido, his son, and his uncle are taken to the concentration camp is only known by implication. Nobody tells anyone, anywhere in the film, that it's because they're Jews. The father never tells his son, during their stay in the camp, "We're here because we're Jews." And the child never hears or realizes, neither from his father nor from the other prisoners or in any other way, that all this is done to his father and to the other inmates because they're Jews.

He doesn't realize this, or at least doesn't say he does, even in hindsight, neither right after his release nor years later, as an adult, looking back on the experience as the film's narrator.

When the mother, Dora, comes to the train station and tries to get her husband and son off the train bound for the concentration camp, she turns to the German officer, and the following dialogue ensues:

OFFICER *(in a German accent)*: Can I help you, Signora?
DORA: There's . . . there's been a mistake.
OFFICER: Mistake? Who are you?
DORA: My husband and my son are on that train.
OFFICER: What's your husband's name?
(He starts looking through papers on the table.)
DORA: Guido Orefice.
(The officer looks quickly at a list and raises his eyes.)
OFFICER: Giosue Orefice and Eliseo Orefice are also on the train. Where is the mistake? There's no mistake.
DORA: I want to get on the train too.

Taking people to a concentration camp is here presented as an arbitrary, absurd, and senseless bureaucratic whim—just like the refusal to grant Guido a permit to open a bookshop was presented in an earlier scene. Dora doesn't say: "There's been a mistake. My husband and son aren't Jewish." She says: "There's been a mistake," simply "a mistake," and the officer checks and sees there hasn't been any mistake—the two are on the list. Hence, those taken to concentration camps are simply those who show up on lists, period. And why do these people and not others show up on the lists? It's unknown and remains so to the end of the film. The thing that's clear is that if your name is on the list, it is a fact you cannot change; your being on the list, for whatever reason, is in itself the reason for your deportation.

And indeed, since none of the prisoners in the concentration camp has even a single trait, whether positive, negative, or neutral, that would distinguish him or her as a Jew, the reason for their being in the camp is clearly not their being Jewish. And it is not presented that way.

It could be that things at the concentration camp are just like they are in town, where, as the father explains to his son earlier in the film, the pastry shop forbids the entry of Jews and dogs, the hardware shop forbids the entry of Spaniards and horses, and the drugstore forbids the entry of Chinese and kangaroos. So here, too, they deported to the camp Jews from places where they don't like Jews, Spaniards from places where they don't like Spaniards, Italians and Chinese from places where they don't like them, and so forth.

And this is the picture actually shown in *Life Is Beautiful*: the Jews are only a small minority among the concentration camp prisoners.

In reality, the Germans marked each inmate with a symbol on his or her uniform: a green triangle for criminals, a red one for political prisoners, a pink triangle for homosexuals, and a red-and-yellow Star of David for Jews. Benigni marked the prisoners in his film in a slightly different way: the Jews have a yellow patch on their clothes; others have a black triangle, the meaning of which is unclear, but it clearly sets them apart from the Jews; there are those whose uniforms bear no marking at all; and also there are those who, unaccountably, don't even wear striped prisoners' uniforms but civilian clothes. In the women's camp, where Dora, Guido's non-Jewish wife, is held, the prisoners have red markings. In the scene in which one of the prisoners is taken to the gas chamber, there are more than ten actresses playing inmates; only one of them bears a yellow mark. Two—Dora herself and the prisoner taken away—bear no marking at all; the rest—that is, the absolute majority—are marked with black triangles.

Thus it's not only that the Jews are a small minority—less than one tenth—of the prisoners in Benigni's concentration camp, but also that the Germans treat them and the other prisoners equally. The Jews don't suffer from any special discrimination. Moreover, the only inmate sent away to the gas chamber is not a Jew.

It could apparently be claimed that, since Dora isn't a Jew, she isn't sent to an actual concentration camp, but to just another adjacent "work camp." This is baseless, because non-Jews were also sent to concentration camps and anyway, were this the case, why does this "work camp" have a Jewish inmate, and why are prisoners there being sent to gas chambers?

And we could also ask: is all this mixing up of markings on uniforms and disregard for historical fact wholly accidental, or is it a consistent and deliberate obscuring, following a distinct logic? A careful viewing of the film, frame by frame, on a home VCR, observing the way the director shows, or, to be accurate, doesn't show—that is, hides—the markings on the prisoners' clothes in the men's camp where Guido is held, clearly reveals that the film was deliberately made this way, with the aim of creating this precise impression in the viewer: that the Jews are a minority among the camp's prisoners.

In the scene where Guido "translates" the German soldier's instructions, which are given inside the prisoners' barracks, only one prisoner, Bartholomew, bears a yellow mark. All the other inmates, and there are dozens of them, were placed by the director, Roberto Benigni—in all the different angles in which the scene was shot—so that the viewers wouldn't be able to see the markings on the uniforms. In stark contrast to what happened in reality in the German concentration camps, some, like Guido himself, are still dressed in civilian clothes, so that it's impossible to tell who among them is Jewish. They were placed so that they hide the prisoners wearing striped uniforms; they, in turn, hide—again, in all of the scene's shooting angles, in long-shot, in medium-shot, and in medium close-up—those behind them, so that their markings, too, are impossible to see. And so on to the back of the barrack. Many of the prisoners even continue to lie comfortably on their bunks throughout the scene, in a way that hides their markings, if they have any, from the camera. Of course, no prisoner in a real German concentration camp would have dared remain lying when the German jailer entered his barrack. He would instantly jump to rigid attention. Anyway, during this whole scene, if because of some tiny camera movement it happens that a colored mark can be seen for a split-second on some prisoner's uniform, it is always a black triangle.

Altogether, in all the scenes taking place in the concentration camp, the number of Jews bearing the yellow mark—including Guido himself—is no more than five. And that's out of surely more than fifty prisoners that the film shows us—in the barrack, at forced labor, and on the way there and back.

So, in the concentration camp as Benigni shows it, and let's recall once again that it is the year 1944, the Jews number less than 10 percent of the prisoners.

In reality, in 1944 and for many years before (the first concentration camps were established in the 1930s, shortly after the Nazis came to power in Germany; the last ones were liberated at the end of the war, in spring 1945), the main reason for sending people from all over Europe to the German concentration camps, and their subsequent torture and killing at these sites, was their being Jews. The Holocaust wasn't an arbitrary, Fascist-bureaucratic hell, which devoured indiscriminately the entire population, as the film might lead us to believe. This specific hell hurt a particular group much harder than the others; it overwhelmingly hurt the Jews in a focused and deliberate manner, and in incomparable, astronomically inverted proportions relative to their percentage of the population of the countries of conquered Europe.

But Benigni obscures this fact, too. From something very specific the Germans did to the Jews, the Holocaust in his film turns into something vague that "bad people" did to "good people." Like in a classic Hollywood Western, his film presents a struggle between "good guys" and "bad guys," at the end of which the ultimate "good guy" appears riding a tank-horse and saves the good boy from the clutches of the baddies.

And we might as well in this context return to the scene where the father explains to his son about the similarity between the pastry shop barring the entrance of Jews and dogs and the hardware store barring the entrance of Spaniards and horses and the drugstore the entrance of Chinese and kangaroos. But the boy wonders: "But we let everyone in!" And Guido answers: "Yeah, well, starting tomorrow, we're going to have a sign too. Who don't you like?" and Giosue responds: "Spiders! And you?" And the father concludes: "Visigoths! And tomorrow we're going to write a sign that says: 'No Spiders or Visigoths Allowed.'"

Guido, that is, Benigni, ostensibly mocks the humiliating racist signs (many of which were indeed posted, even before the war, in German cities, but almost never in Italy), not only forbidding the entrance of Jews but also associating them with dogs, by making up other absurd pairings supposedly barred entrance in other places—Spaniards and horses, Chinese and kangaroos, spiders and Visigoths.

But not all these pairings are alike. In the first three instances, the real one in the pastry shop and the two imaginary instances in the hardware store and the drugstore—the excluded human-animal pairings are comprised of existent peoples (Jews, Spaniards, and Chinese) and of large mammals, moreover mammals that children and adults are particularly fond of (dogs, horses, and kangaroos).

In the last instance, in the sign that Guido-Benigni himself is ostensibly planning to post, the order is reversed: the human half of the pair is preceded by the animal, a spider, a tiny and mostly invisible insect, which nests in small crevices and dark corners, and which moves many people to repulsion, and even terror and phobia—a creature that actually cannot be barred entrance to a shop. The same goes for the people, the Visigoths, a nonexistent, extinct people, who, therefore, it is also impossible to refuse entrance to.

Apparently, Benigni takes the racial laws to absurdity. But why did he choose the Visigoths of all peoples, and spiders of all creatures of the animal kingdom?

The Visigoths, as history books tell us, were a Teutonic people that originated in Scandinavia. In the third century A.D., they migrated southwards, and in the fourth century they converted to Christianity. In the year 410 they conquered Rome, and the Visigoth kingdom became the strongest of those built on the ruins of the Roman Empire. Ultimately—and that's the relevant point for the present discussion—they disappeared, wholly assimilated into the surrounding culture, so that in today's Italian culture there is no trace of theirs.

Is this, by implication, the place Benigni reserves for the Jews in Christian society? Are they supposed to wholly assimilate until they disappear like the Visigoths did, or just hang around on its margins, in cracks and crevices, like tiny insects, not of any greater import than spiders, if not as repulsive and terrifying to some?

I'll say it again: I do not claim nor believe that *Life Is Beautiful* originated in some nonexistent secret council of "the elders of the Vatican"; but still, it's worth noting how much this film is compatible with the Catholic Church's attitude toward the Jews and the Holocaust.

Life Is Beautiful was ranked one of the best ten films of 1998 recommended to the faithful by the United States Conference of Catholic Bishops. Pope John Paul II, who only watches films with a "religious content," reportedly saw the film in a private screening in the Vatican in Benigni's company and was unofficially quoted as saying that "this film makes you think . . . even there, in this concentration camp, you could find saints."[4]

Which is a curious choice of words indeed. For who but the Holy See should know that saints can by definition only be true believers, that is, Catholics and never Jews, as Guido is supposed to be.

The Catholic priest Maksymilian Kolbe and the Carmelite nun Edith Stein (who was born Jewish but converted to Catholicism) were both killed by the Nazis in Auschwitz. John Paul II canonized Kolbe and beatified Stein as official, martyred saints—they alone of all the victims of the Holocaust. Unlike Benigni's Guido or William Styron's Sophie, Kolbe and Stein were real people, who bravely underwent great spiritual and physical tortures for their faith before being murdered. (Oscar Schindler, who was awarded Israel's Righteous among the Nations medal, demonstrated rare courage, generosity, determination, and resourcefulness during the Holocaust, risking his life many times, and motivated by simple decency and humanity. His story by all means deserves to serve as example for the world, and he did become the hero of a successful film, because Hollywood, as mentioned, will digest Holocaust films as long as they are centered on Christian heroes. But even though a Catholic by birth, Schindler never fulfilled the requirements of official Church sainthood—he didn't (1) die for the faith and (2) perform miracles.)

But isn't there something a little odd about this tendency, common to both Hollywood and the Catholic Church, to emphasize and glorify the heroism and suffering of the Holocaust's Christian victims—a kind of "creeping annexation" of the Holocaust, which retroactively turns it, ever so imperceptibly, at the expense of historical truth, into a myth of Christian martyrdom? We may note that the site of Kolbe and Stein's death has become a center of pilgrimage, so much so that some of the pilgrims honestly don't understand "what the Jews have to do with Auschwitz"—a place as worthy as any, in their opinion, to be put under the sign of the crucifix.

Roberto Benigni's film, surprisingly or not, seamlessly merges into a larger psychological and ideological trend, a trend whose purpose isn't only to whitewash the unforgivable silence of Pope Pius XII during the Holocaust but also to stress that it was not only the Jews but the Christians as well who suffered persecution by the Nazis. This is coupled with the refusal to admit outright the cardinal, decisive influence of the Church, in its various branches, on the development of traditional anti-Semitism, sowing for centuries the seeds that grew into the phenomenon of the Jew as the scapegoat and object of hatred of an entire civilization. The same civilization that went stark raving mad during the first half of the twentieth century. The same hatred that reached its dark zenith in Auschwitz.

And what about the modern, virulent version of traditional anti-Semitism, the Nazi-Fascist "race theory," which, with iron conclusiveness, led to the extermination of Jews with gas—the same gas originally produced for the extermination of domestic pests? Benigni apparently mocks it as well by impersonating the Fascist Ministry of Education inspector, stripping in front of a group of schoolchildren and explaining to them, with a live demonstration on his not exactly dazzling form, the splendors of the Aryan race.

"I've just come from Rome, right this minute," he says, "to tell you in order that you'll know, children, that our race is a superior one. I was chosen, I was, by racist Italian scientists in order to demonstrate how superior our race is."

And then, as the script says, "In a flash, he jumps up on the table to show the children how handsome he is." Standing on the table, "Inspector" Guido-Benigni continues: "Why did they pick me, children? Must I tell you? Where can you find someone more handsome than me?" And he goes on to illustrate his claim with the help of different parts of his body—from his ear to his belly button.

This entire scene mocking racial theory is based on the contradiction between the way the fake "inspector" presents himself as a breathtakingly handsome person, an exemplary superior Aryan, and the fact that the actor playing him is far from being conventionally handsome or physically perfect. In fact, his appearance is quite unlikely to have been accepted by even the most bungling Nazi scientist as an ideal model of the Master Race.

The scene's effectiveness depends, in short, on the ridiculous situation in which Benigni, whose physical appearance is not the one classically associated with Roman gods or with irresistible bodily charm, explains to the children how handsome he is and how perfect he looks. Meaning—"Look, children, what an idiotic idea this whole racial theory is. It considers the obviously malformed as handsome to the point of perfection."

Only in the fictive reality of *Life Is Beautiful*, Benigni isn't Benigni. He isn't standing on a theater stage as a long-nosed Italian stand-up artist with a less than perfect appearance, jauntily mocking the silliness of racial theory. Neither is he a Christian Italian, bravely making fun of racial theory and using himself as an example for how ugly both he and racism are. In the film, Roberto Benigni is supposed to play the role of a Jew. Hence, in this scene, even when the character he plays impersonates a fascist inspector, the one who is ostensibly ridiculing the theory of race is the ridiculed Jew himself. The joke is actually on him.

And what does this ridicule really mean, as it is presented in the film? It means that this Jew, who only pretends to be an Aryan, is exactly as ugly as the scientists adhering to race theory claim he is. Thus, the result is that Benigni doesn't really ridicule their obscene theory. On the contrary, he actually reaffirms and reinforces it.

In light of all this, it's no wonder that this Jew as conceived by Benigni becomes a victim who is sacrificed on the altar of his Jewishness.

But he is not an innocent victim of absurd hatred and ugly intolerance, as he may appear to be at first glance. The altar he is sacrificed on in this film is an altogether different one.

NOTES

1. As detailed, for instance, in Lenni Yahil, *The Holocaust: The Fate of Europe's Jews 1932–1945* (in Hebrew) (Israel: Yad Vashem and Schoken Publishing, 1987).

2. Dan Vittorio Segre, *Memoirs of a Fortunate Jew* (London: Peter Halban Publishing, 1987).

3. *Sophie's Choice*, script and director: Alan J. Pakula, based on a story by William Styron, United States 1982.

4. *New York Post*, February 5, 1999.

Chapter 5

Annihilation as Salvation

Very close to the ending of *Life Is Beautiful,* immediately before the Germans run away and the Americans arrive, the protagonist is executed. Roberto Benigni (with his cowriter Vincenzo Cerami) decided that Guido must die, and at this particular timing.

Why did he make this decision? Why didn't Benigni allow his Guido to survive the concentration camp and go on living happily with his loving family after the war, the way he allowed Guido's wife Dora and their son Giosue? The answer, on the face of it, is that Guido sacrifices his life to save his son. But what actually happens in the film doesn't support this assertion.

The scene sequence leading to Guido's death proceeds as follows: the concentration camp is in chaos. Guido jumps from his bed to see what is happening. Bartholomew explains to Guido, "The war's over. They [the Germans] are running away." Guido sees the Germans loading prisoners onto trucks and asks Bartholomew, "Where are the trucks going?" to which Bartholomew gives the charged response, "They leave full and come back empty. Where do you think they're going?"

Guido says to Bartholomew, "We should get out of here." And so he takes Giosue and, leaving the barrack, hides the child inside a small metal hut in the camp yard. He runs to the women's camp, but then returns to his son's hiding place, takes a blanket, and before leaving the child again, he warns him that "if I should be a little late," he must stay hidden until it's all over—until all the Germans are gone and "it is absolutely quiet and you can't see anyone for miles."

Curiously, he doesn't say something like "Wait for me here, and don't come out until I'm back." His choice of words makes it clear, at least to the viewers, that Guido is preparing his son for the eventuality that he, his father, won't return. That is, it seems that unlike the child, he's already taken the time to read the script and knows what is about to happen.

Guido wraps the blanket around him to make it look like a dress and runs back to the women's camp. There he frantically searches for his wife Dora among the trucks loaded with prisoners and the empty barracks, but he doesn't find her. Then the Germans spot him, capture him, and subsequently take him away and execute him. Afterward, the remaining Germans are seen leaving the camp, and the last of the prisoners exit the barracks and leave as well. Giosue then comes out from his hiding place to find in front of him the liberating American tank, which he is convinced he has won in the game his father made up for him.

In this sequence of screen events, there's no evidence that the father has given his life to save the life of his son, no causal or circumstantial link whatever between the death of the father and the survival of the boy. He may have saved his son's life by hiding him in the metal hut, but there is no connection between his later actions and his son's coming through alive. The script didn't create a situation in which the father must sacrifice his life to save his son, and so he doesn't.

So this is not a story about a father who gives his life for the sake of his son; it's a different story. And the question remains: why did Benigni take Guido's life if the script's narrative logic didn't require it to save the little boy?

At second thought, it may seem that Guido dies in a last-minute attempt to reach his wife in the women's camp and save her. But his actions in his last moments seem utterly senseless not only in regard to narrative logic but also, and perhaps most of all, in regard to their human probability. Instead of guarding his six-year-old child—whom he defended devotedly throughout their imprisonment in the concentration camp—and protecting him to the very last moment, he suddenly leaves him alone, just at the moment when it could endanger both his and the boy's life. Instead, minutes before their liberation, he loses his patience and goes on a hopeless rescue mission dressed as a woman, attempting to reunite with his wife right before the Germans flee and he, his son, and perhaps his wife as well are about to be saved.

Why is Guido so anxious to abandon at this precise moment his small son, whose life is still in danger, and run off looking for his wife? The obvious answer is that love drives him to it, because this is a romantic comedy. But why do Guido's love and concern for his wife suddenly swell so wildly in him that they exceed his love and concern for his son?

There is one plausible explanation, surprising at first, but actually almost unavoidable: when you repeatedly watch this scene sequence, examining its narrative logic and especially remembering the outcome of Guido's odd behavior in his last moments, it becomes more and more apparent that Guido seems to be doing everything he can so as not to get out of the concentration camp alive.

Guido pushes his luck. He avidly courts danger. That is to say—as often happens to certain people, who tend to act recklessly when facing extreme danger—he may be looking for his death. Consciously or not, Guido may have decided, for some reason, to get himself killed.

Starting when he hides his son in the metal hut and ending in his death, Guido goes to considerable lengths so that the Nazis—who are naturally very busy saving their own lives—spot him and capture him. And his effort pays off; they duly spot and capture him. And so, at the end of the film, on the very threshold of salvation, Guido finds what he has really been looking for.

But why, if we accept this psychological explanation for his behavior, does he decide to kill himself? Why, at least, does he seem to be doing all he can to get into trouble at the last moment? His behavior doesn't have, as we have seen, a reasonable cause arising naturally from the film's plot. The survival of Dora and Giosue isn't made possible by his death. And anyway, it's obviously not Guido himself, the imaginary character, but Benigni and Cerami, the scriptwriters who imagined him, who decided, not even bothering to make up some feasible reason for it, that Guido won't survive the concentration camp.

But again, why? Why does the film have to end with the father's death and the reunification of the surviving mother and son, and not, for instance, with the death of the child, or the mother, or all three, or none?

The first and obvious answer is that the combination of one dead and two alive, out of a family of three, is the correct formula for creating a moving, cleansing ending for any film, especially a romantic comedy set in a concentration camp. In a two-to-one for the side-of-life outcome, there is happiness mingled with sorrow, mirth with pain, victory with partial defeat—a bittersweet, not entirely perfect happy ending, which—from the viewer emotional-manipulation point of view—is the true perfect happy ending, as the film's success amply testifies.

Two-to-one for life is the best result that a film like this could present, and it is perhaps the only one the audience would buy. We could safely bet, based on long past experience in popular cinema, that had the film ended with death triumphing—a round naught-to-three or even a disappointing one-to-two—most moviegoers would tend to be disappointed, and Roberto Benigni would perhaps not have had the opportunity to jump on the back of chairs all over the world and declare that "life is beautiful." On the other hand, if life were to win three-naught and all three were to survive their concentration camp adventure, most moviegoers would probably be unwilling to accept the outcome. It might have seemed kitschy and exaggerated, improbable and extremely unrealistic; and this would clearly also hurt the film's sentimental and box-office appeal.

Based on this reasoning, Benigni and Cerami probably didn't have much choice but to kill one of the three family members at the end of the film. But still, why did they choose to sacrifice Guido's life to achieve their bittersweet happy ending?

The script evidently couldn't kill Giosue, for how could one accept the death of a small child, one of the two main protagonists, as the fit ending for any popular film, let alone a romantic comedy—in which this death, moreover, must be combined with the genre's obligatory happy ending?

But, on the other hand, it would certainly be possible to kill the mother instead of the father. In most viewers' opinion, would the moving effect of the ending be lost somehow, had the mother been the one to die at the end of the film? Most likely it would not. On the contrary, it would make for some sort of human as well as poetic justice that the father, and not the mother, would be spared and come out with his little boy to a new, free life after the Holocaust experience they'd been through. He has put so much love and creative effort into saving his son while she has been mostly absent from the story. Indeed, the script never gave her a chance to contribute anything to the saving of her son.

And yet the script chose to kill the father. We should therefore delve deeper to see what narrative end or other objective the father's death serves, which the mother's death couldn't.

As mentioned, *Life Is Beautiful* is a romantic comedy of the ethnic-class sub-genre. But what stands in the way of Guido and Dora's love is not just the difference in their social class—his being poor and belonging to the common people and her being a rich "princess"—but also, and perhaps mainly, the religious or racial difference: he is a Jew and she is a Christian, and the plot takes place, lest we forget, at a time in which Jews are considered officially, by law, to be an inferior race or worse. The Christian Dora escapes with her Jewish beloved right from the arms of her fiancé, a Christian and very respectable fascist citizen. Following this incident—as we are informed, in a scene occurring years later, in which a meeting between Dora's mother and her grandson Giosue takes place in his father's bookshop—the mother cuts off all ties with her daughter, shuns her new family, and, for six long years, renounces her grandson, born of this forbidden union.

Does Dora's mother reject her daughter and grandson just because the daughter defied her will and didn't marry the man that the mother meant for her? Or is it because the daughter chose a lower-class, poor man instead?

No. The film itself gives an explicit answer to this in the scene of Dora's escape with her beloved Guido from under the nose of her fiancé. During her engagement party, in which Guido serves as a waiter, Dora slides under the table, kisses Guido who is looking for the cookies he dropped there, and tells him: "Take me away!" Guido exits and comes back riding his uncle's horse, gets her on the horse, and to the astonishment of the celebrating crowd, the two make a galloping escape from the engagement party to create a family of their own. The horse they escape on bears the conspicuous inscription "Attention, Jewish horse," smeared on it in an earlier scene by anti-Semitic thugs.

What the film's creators are glaringly saying here is that Guido and Dora's audacity, the astonishment of her social class, and the mother's rejection of the daughter and her new family all stem from one source—the fact that Guido is a Jew. The explanation is writ large on the horse on whose back Guido "abducts" Dora from her "rightful place," from her intended husband, her social class, her religion, and her race. This is the reason for the mother's rejection of

her daughter and the grandchild she bore—because she married a
Jew.

Nevertheless, later in the film, the alienated grandmother appears
out of the blue, after years of rejection and silence, in her son-in-
law's bookshop—making sure first that he himself is not present—
to see her grandson and tell him and his mother that she'll come
tomorrow to celebrate his sixth birthday. (By the way, the child's exact age isn't spelled out in the film, although in all versions of the
script his age is expressly stated as six. But if so, by basic arithmetic,
one arrives at one of two conclusions: either the boy was born before
his parents ever met—because their meeting occurs, as the film does
state, in the summer of 1939—or World War II went on at least until
1946.)

Why does this happen now? Why on the eve of his sixth birthday,
not the third, or the eighth? Why does the grandmother suddenly
decide to forgive her daughter and acknowledge her grandson after
this long estrangement? What makes her change her mind? The film
provides no answers of any sort for these questions.

On the face of it, it is unclear what narrative need Benigni and Cerami meant to fulfill by adding the scene of the grandmother's encounter with the grandson. Why was it important for Benigni to
include this episode? What does the fact that the grandmother has
reconciled with the mother and grandson add to the viewers' understanding of the film or their enjoyment of it? The film's plot
could seemingly progress very well without this scene, with no detectable loss. But since it has been included in the film, it must have
some kind of meaning.

And its meaning lies in the cinematic syntax—the precise script
sequence in which the scene is positioned. In the chain of screen
events, the reconciliation scene doesn't take place on the eve of Giosue's sixth birthday, which is its ostensible excuse, but, as a matter
of fact, on the eve of Guido and Giosue's deportation to the concentration camp. Right after the bookshop reconciliation between the
grandmother and grandchild scene, we see Dora driving to bring
her mother to celebrate together Giosue's birthday. But when the
two women return to Dora's home, they find the house in disarray,
the furniture smashed, and Guido and Giosue gone.

The inescapable conclusion is that it was important for the
scriptwriters that Dora and her mother get reconciled precisely at
this stage, before her husband and son are taken to the concentration

camp. That's the only possible explanation for the grandmother's sudden change of heart, which doesn't contribute anything at all to the narrative. (The grandmother could simply not show up at all, not here and not anywhere else in the film; Dora could just as easily come back home by herself and find her husband and son gone, and the story could go on exactly the way it does from that point on.)

What was essential for the scriptwriters, therefore, was that Dora and her mother make up before the Holocaust segment of the film, and that the viewers know about this reconciliation and see it.

But to what end? What does it add to the story? Does it have anything to do with the ending—with the father's eventual death? Or the mother and son's survival? Maybe it has something to do with Guido's Jewishness? With the fact that Giosue and Dora are not Jews?

Yes, indeed. Dora starts the film and ends it as a Christian. She doesn't convert, for instance, when she marries Guido, and later, when she voluntarily goes with her husband and son to the concentration camp although her name is not on the deportation list, it isn't out of any identification with the suffering of the persecuted Jews; her decision to join them is presented as arising from love and a purely personal identification with and devotion to her beloved family.

Giosue, Guido and Dora's son, could be considered a Jew (a "half-Jew," or *mischlige*, to be precise) according to the Nazi Racial Laws, but not according to any other known criterion. He is not Jewish according to the *Halakhah*, which defines a Jew as someone born to a Jewish mother or converted; he fulfills neither condition. Giosue isn't Jewish in his father's eyes; Guido, as mentioned, doesn't raise his son as a Jew and never tells him, in any part of the film, that he is a Jew. Neither is he a Jew, of course, in his mother's eyes, and she doesn't raise him as one. And most importantly, Giosue doesn't for a moment view himself as a Jew—not before he is taken with his father to the concentration camp, not during his imprisonment there with others who are supposedly Jewish, and not later—neither right after his release nor years later, when, as an adult, he narrates the film for us.

Neither as a child nor as an adult, for the entire film, before, during, and after the Holocaust, does Giosue live, or perceive himself, as a Jew.

The Germans deport him to a concentration camp, so the viewers tend to automatically assume that Giosue is Jewish, but, as we have

seen in the last chapter, this assumption has no basis in the film itself. Nowhere is it said that he is a Jew or that that's the reason for
his being taken to the camp. It is not even clear whether he is imprisoned because his father is a Jew, or whether the other inmates
are there because they are Jewish. On the contrary, none of the prisoners, just like Giosue himself, have any Jewish attributes, and, just
like him, they too don't show, for the entire film, any sign that they
consider themselves Jews.

In the reality of the Nazi era, the overwhelming majority of the people whom the Germans deported to the concentration camps were
Jews. As we have seen in earlier chapters, this fact is all but invisible
in the film's reality. Hence the seemingly reasonable assumption—
that if the child is sent by the Germans to a concentration camp, then
he must be Jewish—is fundamentally mistaken. It is in complete dis-
agreement with what actually happens in the film.

As viewers, especially as Israeli and Jewish viewers, we do here
what psychologists call "cognitive completion": since we know that
in reality, most of those who were sent to concentration camps were
Jewish, we assume Giosue is Jewish as well, even though the film
doesn't once give support to such an assumption.

As a side note, I'd like to mention that in at least three translations
that I've seen (the film's Hebrew subtitles, and its script in Hebrew
and in English) the translators—probably unintentionally—mislead
the viewers by automatically translating Giosue's name into the
original biblical name it derives from, Yehoshua in Hebrew or
Joshua in English; this could have strengthened the viewers' misim-
pression that the child is Jewish.

But the boy isn't an Israeli Jew named Yehoshua, and neither is he
a British or American Jew named Joshua. The boy's name is Giosue,
and he is a non-Jewish Italian child whose mother in the film isn't
Jewish either; only his father is portrayed, indirectly, as "Jewish."
And at the end of the film, the only member of the family labeled a
Jew dies. The two other family members are saved and miraculously
reunited, and thus we finally discover the film's true moral.

The film's uplifting conclusion is reached not by the dead Jew, but
by his surviving Christian family. They are the ones who, at the end
of the adventure, discover that "life is beautiful." Life is beautiful,
but not for Jews.

The film presents the mother and son's meeting and reunification
as a wonderful, tremendous victory, a true happy ending that the

Jewish father's recent death does nothing at all to darken in any way whatsoever.

This is how the film ends:

The American tank Giosue is riding moves on a dirt road, on both sides of which liberated prisoners, in their striped uniforms, are walking. Suddenly Giosue recognizes someone in the crowd. He shouts.

GIOSUE *(yelling)*: Mommy!
(The tank stops. The child jumps down and races back up the hill as fast as he can.)
GIOSUE *(yelling)*: Mommy!
(Running, he throws himself at his mother, who is sitting on the grass near a cherry tree. She falls backward, Giosue on top of her, kissing her.)
DORA: Giosue!
GIOSUE: We won!
DORA: Yes, we won!
GIOSUE: A thousand points! Couldn't you just die laughing? We came in first! We get to take the tank home! We won!
(The mother lifts her son in her arms. The child is laughing, she is laughing. The frame freezes.)
THE END.

It's not only that the death of Guido, the father and husband, doesn't cast even a tiny cloud over his beloved wife and son's rejoicing; they don't even mention him at the moment of their great victory. As if he hasn't been murdered just moments ago, or even as though he never existed. He is simply obliterated. Perhaps they do not know for certain that he is dead, but the mother doesn't even ask where he is, and the child doesn't wonder where he's gone either. The mother and son celebrating their victory obliterate the father's memory.

Benigni's choosing to end the film this way, a few minutes after Guido is murdered by a German soldier behind a wall, creates for the viewer a very problematic chain of emotional experiences, leading as it does straight from the rightful grief over the death of the film's protagonist—who is such a likable guy—to the sublime happiness of the mother and son and the great joy of their salvation. Indeed these two, so soon after the husband and father's execution, act not only as if they were indifferent to his death but also perhaps even as if celebrating it. The result is that this obliterated, hidden, futile death is actually an inseparable part of the great euphoria of liberation, as if it caused them relief and solved a problem for them, no less so than the American tanks.

Let's imagine for a moment that at the end of that hypothetical film discussed earlier, taking place during the horrors of Apartheid, the black father were taken to a hidden spot and killed there, out of our sight, and right afterward the white mother and son would be released and reunited, cheerful as ever, without shedding a tear for his death nor mentioning his name or even the fact that he had ever existed. It would be as if the film's creator were telling us, "Everything's all right, problem solved and over with, the nigger's out of our way, life is beautiful, go back about your business."

The sequence of emotional experiences in the closing scenes of *Life Is Beautiful* is constructed in such a way that one could easily err and feel as though it is the father's death that enables the wholesome re-unification of the mother and son. In other words, it is as though it's the fact that the Jew hasn't survived that allows the Christians to live happily ever after the Holocaust.

It seems that Benigni himself felt some discomfort about ending his film this way. Perhaps this is why he inserted an additional voiceover in this scene—probably after the film's completion, as an afterthought, because it doesn't appear in the original script. It is the voice of the adult Giosue, who serves as the film's narrator: "This is my story. This is the sacrifice my father made. This was his gift to me."

But these belatedly inserted words of the adult Giosue not only fail to tone down the wholehearted justification of the father's death, implicit in the film's final scene, but they also actually reinforce it. For here is the orphaned son, after presumably growing older and wiser, portraying his father's life and death not as a loss and a tragedy, not as a crime and a wound that will never heal, but just as a "gift and a sacrifice" made by the father himself so that his wife and son could reunite and live on.

Hence, the role of the Jew in this story is to die of his own accord to allow for the happy end. His death is not presented here as a murder, which presupposes a murderer and thus places the blame squarely on another, particular individual, nor is it presented as an accident or a mistake, where, for all the grief and pain, no one is to blame except for blind fate. Instead, it is presented—it should be carefully noted—as a "self"-sacrifice. And that, naturally, depends on the free will and initiative of the person who decides to make the sacrifice, so actually no one's to blame, not even fate. He was the one who did it.

Following this noble "sacrifice" (sacrifice in quotation marks, for, as we have seen, Guido did not have any real need to die for the sake of his wife and son, who were saved anyway; the script sacrificed him, and for another purpose altogether), the mother and son are reunited—this time, without a Jew in the family.

And this joyful reunion also retroactively explains the meaning of the scene of reconciliation between Dora and her mother, just prior to the Holocaust.

According to the formula of the subgenre—a social-ethnic romantic comedy, as it is applied in this film—a man and a woman from different social classes (and in this case, different religions and races as well) fall in love, but the family of the higher class and race's lover strongly opposes the love affair, let alone the marriage. The loving couple gets married anyway and, in spite of the family's resistance (in this case, that of Dora's mother) and to their great displeasure, creates a new "mixed" family, that is, they have a child.

Eventually, in all films in this genre, the bride's family realizes that the unwanted bridegroom (who is, e.g., Mid-Eastern, poor, black, Jewish, Eskimo, or Indian) is a good man after all, a devoted husband, and a wonderful father. Therefore the family regrets its opposition to the marriage, reconciles with the daughter, and accepts the marriage, the son-in-law, and his "inferior" relatives, and they all become one big happy family.

Not in this film. Here, the second part of the predictable, tried-and-true formula doesn't play as expected. It doesn't get the chance to. Because right before the happy reconciliation, the Holocaust suddenly crashes in and spoils the party. Seconds before Dora's mother is going to meet—after six years of boycott and estrangement—and reconcile with her daughter's Jewish husband, the Germans take him and his son to the concentration camp.

But this is only how things seem to be happening. There is certainly another way to view this turn of events: the Holocaust doesn't spoil the party at all, on the contrary, it solves the problem. Dora's Christian mother rejects her daughter because she married a Jew. For six years or more she doesn't speak to her, doesn't see her daughter or her grandson. Suddenly, for no special reason, she declares that she wants to make up and reconcile. But then, just before the meeting with the Jewish son-in-law, a *force majeure*, a superior force sent by the superior race, breaks in and takes her son-in-law and her grandson to a concentration camp, thus preventing at the last moment the grudging acceptance of the Jew who infiltrated the family.

Lo and behold, the very same superior force, that *deus ex machina* that prevented the unavoidable but unpalatable acceptance of the Jew in the middle of the film, intervenes again toward the film's end and kills the Jew who seemed for a moment as if he was going to get out of this one, too. And now, after finally being rid of the Jew who guilefully penetrated it, the family can be truly reconciled. The daughter and grandson will no doubt return to the arms of the Christian mother-grandmother—who ostensibly wanted to make up with them earlier, but unhappily couldn't—and everything will come back to its rightful, natural order.

By the way, one of the students in the class in which I taught this film interpreted the plot based on his understanding that the grandmother, Dora's mother, was the one who informed the Germans that her son-in-law was Jewish and caused him to be sent to the concentration camp, not realizing that her grandson would be sent there, too, and her daughter would follow as well. "For, how could the grandmother show up in the bookstore right after the father was taken from there," that student wondered, "if she didn't have a foreknowledge of his arrest—that is, if she wasn't the one who brought it about?"

Excellent question. In my opinion, the film itself doesn't provide enough proof for us to deduce that this is what happened. On the other hand, the film provides no proof to refute such a deduction or make it inconceivable.

In any event, it's important to note that Dora's mother, who will surely be very happy to welcome her daughter and grandson back from the dead, never actually accepted her Jewish son-in-law, never knew him, and never shook his hand or talked to him. The Holocaust, from her point of view, is not a catastrophe; it is a solution.

In *Life Is Beautiful*, the Holocaust of the Jews serves as the final solution to the film's main dilemma—a Christian woman of high birth falls in love with a Jew, a member of the loathsome race. The Holocaust solves the problem by eliminating the Jew, and there you have a perfect, 100 percent, unalloyed happy ending.

But, it should be again stressed, it wasn't the Holocaust that killed Guido. The scriptwriter who created him also eliminated him. That way Benigni (together with Cerami) killed two birds, or to be exact, two Jews (Uncle Elisio also died, of course) with one stone. He both "solved" the film's main plot dilemma and "carried out" in an artistic-cinematic way what the Nazis endeavored to do in practice. For in the end, the scriptwriter-director kills the Jew a moment before he manages to escape from the imaginary concentration camp Benigni built, and he saves the two Christians who were "mistakenly" deported there. This seems to be the final verdict of *Life Is Beautiful*: those who "deserve to" die, and those who "deserve to" live on.

And if the story of this particular family is really a parable, as the narrator tells us at the start of the film, here is one way to understand its moral: Christian Europe is better off with its Jews, like the Visigoths, gone forever or, at most, banished like spiders; and then the rest can live on undisturbed, in peace and quiet, happily ever after.

If we agree to this interpretation of the film, we should also admit a decoding of *Life Is Beautiful* as not only an "artistic" form of denial of the reality of the Holocaust but also as a meta-argument justifying it.

Chapter 6

Gift and Sacrifice

The names of protagonists, like any detail in a book, a film, or any other work of art, are almost never accidental. In most cases, when naming a fictional character, the writer, consciously or not, chooses a name that has special resonance and meaning for him or her.

In the case of *Life Is Beautiful*, scriptwriters Benigni and Cerami themselves emphasize the importance of names in the scene in which Guido and his friend Ferruccio arrive for the first time at the upholsterer's where Ferruccio is to be employed. During the ensuing conversation Guido asks the upholsterer, "What do you think of the political situation?" At that exact moment the man yells at his children, who are misbehaving in the background: "Benito! Adolfo! Behave!" From that, of course, Guido as well as the viewers may infer that the upholsterer is an ardent Fascist, having named his children after Mussolini and Hitler. (And the glaring answer to the political question, even though it isn't expressly answered, is, of course, that "Benito and Adolfo" *are* misbehaving.)

Hence, Benigni himself lets us understand that the names people give to their children, and presumably those that writers give to their protagonists, are carriers of meaning and significance. That said, we can try to find out the possible significance of "Giosue," the name Benigni gave to the child protagonist of *Life Is Beautiful*.

What is the meaning of the Italian name "Giosue"? Ostensibly, as it appeared in the English and Hebrew subtitles of the film, it is the Italian equivalent of the Hebrew name "Yehoshua," or Joshua in English. But practically—in Italian language and culture—Giosue is synonymous with "Jesus"; that is, another name for Christ.

Furthermore, though the spelling of the two names is quite different—Jesus is spelled Gesu, while Yehoshua is spelled Giosue—they're pronounced very similarly. Gesu is pronounced "Je-zoo" and Giosue is pronounced "Jo-zoo-eh."

In the Italian *Great Book of Names,* these two names are explained:

> Gesu—a translation of the Hebrew name Yehoshua, meaning savior. Being the name of the Christian messiah, it is almost nonexistent as a first name in Italy, not in use out of respect and reverence, while quite common in Spain (Jesus), as well as in English speaking countries (Joshua).
>
> Giosue—from the Hebrew, Yeho-Shua, meaning "God the savior," and in short Gesu, the savior. A common name among Jews in ancient times, also common today in Spain. In the Bible Joshua was the successor of Moses, and led the Israelites into the promised land.[1]

Both Gesu and Giosue are uncommon in Italy. Gesu doesn't exist at all as a first name, and Giosue is exceedingly rare.

Still, were Italian parents to name their child Giosue, their family and neighbors would most likely understand this as naming him after Jesus Christ. No one would probably suspect that they named the child after the biblical Joshua, the son of Nun, leader of the Hebrews, successor of Moses, and conqueror of Canaan.

In Italian language and culture, the two names are one. Giosue is Gesu, and Joshua is Jesus. This semantic sameness is justified historically and etymologically. Jesus's original name was Yeshua, not a name in itself in Hebrew but a shortened version of Yehoshua. The meaning of the two names is identical as well, or at least they represent the same idea—"savior," or "he who brings salvation from God."

Thus, whether he did it consciously or not, Benigni gave his child protagonist a name loaded with significance—he named him after Jesus Christ, no less.

We can, therefore, justifiably construe Giosue in *Life Is Beautiful* as Jesus of Nazareth or perhaps his modern incarnation. Christians believe Jesus, who rose from the dead three days after his crucifixion, will come back again at the end of days, this time to bring heaven on earth and salvation to all true believers. In *Life Is Beautiful* he comes back in 1939 as Giosue, son of the Jewish Guido and the Christian Dora.

In the New Testament, we are told of Mary, who becomes pregnant with a baby who is not her husband Joseph's but the son of

God.[2] Like Jesus, son of Mary, Giosue in the film is also to all intents and purposes the son of a Jewish man, but he is "born" on screen in an unnatural way, with no hint of sexual union or even a pregnancy. Giosue just suddenly appears, in a brilliant cinematic trick. After Guido and Dora arrive at the uncle's house, Dora enters the greenhouse in the garden and disappears. Guido follows her and disappears as well, and the next moment a six-year-old child pops out of the greenhouse, who turns out to be their son; this is how he's "born" in the film: miraculously, as if out of the blue.

According to the New Testament, the evil King Herod learned about the coming birth of Jesus the messiah and immediately set out to kill him. But an angel warned Joseph and instructed him to run away to Egypt and hide the young child there until Herod's death, and so Joseph did. But when Herod learned that Jesus the messiah was being hidden from him, he "sent forth and slew all the [Jewish] children that were in Bethlehem, from two years old under," believing Jesus to be among them.

In *Life Is Beautiful,* Giosue's enemies first try to stop him from being born by preventing his parents' marriage. When he's born anyway, the king's henchmen, this time in the guise of Hitler's troops, again attempt to kill little Giosue, by killing all Jewish (according to Nazi law) children and their parents. The entire German extermination machine almost seems to have one sole purpose—to annihilate little Giosue. As Guido tells him, toward the end of the film: "You should see how angry they are, how they're looking for you!"

But if Giosue, in this interpretation, is cast in the role of Jesus, who is Guido? Outwardly, he is Giosue's father, like Joseph the carpenter who functioned outwardly as the father of young Jesus. But the two stories are not identical, of course. In the New Testament, Joseph's sole role is to be a companion to Mary and save Jesus from King Herod, that is, to take him abroad and keep him there until the danger is over. In *Life Is Beautiful,* despite numerous ominous signs of the German intention to kill all Jews, Guido is in no hurry to hide Giosue and make him safe from their wrath. So the child is captured by his persecutors and taken to the very heart of danger. Once there, Guido does make an effort to save him, and the boy is indeed saved.

In the New Testament, the forces of evil attempt to destroy Jesus twice. In the first instance, which occurs in his infancy, when they find out about the birth of the messiah, Joseph saves him. The second time happens in his adulthood, after he already has a wide following among the people. In their stubborn refusal to accept him as the messiah, they succeed in killing him; one of his friends and disciples, Judas Iscariot, betrays him for thirty pieces of silver and turns him in for crucifixion.

In which of these two stories from the founding of Christianity can we find, if not an exact parallel, then a powerfully suggestive correlation to the story about Jesus-Giosue's attempted murder at the concentration camp—the story of Jesus's attempted murder in infancy, or his betrayal by a disciple and subsequent crucifixion? Again, the names seem to hold the answer.

The name of the first prisoner whom Guido and Giosue meet in the concentration camp is Bartholomew, after one of the twelve apostles (his Hebrew name was Bar-Thalmai), who accompanied the adult Jesus until his crucifixion and later continued to spread his gospel. And Bartholomew does serve as a tutor and guide to both father and son—especially to Giosue.

And what about Guido? If Giosue is another name for Jesus, what does the father's name mean?

It should perhaps be noted in passing that there existed a real historical figure by the name of Guido of Arezzo, a Benedictine monk (c. 995–1050) who, according to the *Catholic Encyclopedia,* "invented the system of staff-notation still in use, and rendered various other services to the progress of musical art and science."[3] But as far as I can see, Benigni's protagonist does not seem to allude to or have any connection with his historical namesake.

Of all male names in the Italian language, including those derived from the Hebrew Bible and the New Testament, the name closest in spelling to Guido is Giuda, which is Italian for Judas. The difference in pronunciation between the two names is considerable, but the spelling is similar enough. That is to say, the father's name in the film is very similar, at least in its spelling, to the name of Judas Iscariot, the traitor-disciple who turned Jesus in to the elders of the Jews, who handed him over to the Romans, thus bringing about the death by crucifixion of the messiah.

The Jewish people, to this day, take their name from that of the tribe of Yehuda (Juda), who was the son of Jacob, one of the three mythic patriarchs. Since biblical times, up to this day, a region in the land of Israel is named Judea and Jews, mostly in Israel, often name their sons Yehuda—after the son of Jacob or another national hero, Yehuda Maccabaeus, leader of the Hasmonean rebellion against the

Syrian Greeks, or after Rabbi Yehuda Hanassi, editor of the *Mishna,* the important Jewish religious text on which the Talmud is based. "Yehuda," in short, in the Hebrew original, is a well-liked, common first name, no less respectable than any other male given name.

Things are obviously different in European languages. "Judas" is never a respectable first name, nor even a neutral one, as it is in the original. In fact, it is not a name at all but is used solely as an un-varyingly negative, hostile epithet meaning "despised traitor"—after the disciple who sold Jesus for thirty pieces of silver. No Christian parents, anywhere in the world, would give their son this wretched name.

Here is the entry in *The Great Book of Names,* for the Italian name Giuda (Judas):

> In the Bible, a son of Jacob and leader of the tribe of Juda, named after him, and the Maccabaeus who led the Jews to victory against the king of Syria. Became a despised name, as it was the name of Iscariot who sold Jesus for thirty pieces of silver, and ever since became a synonym for traitor. Nonetheless, it has remained in use among Jews.

Giosue, an extremely rare name that is almost never used, is the closest Italian name to Gesu, or Jesus (which, as mentioned earlier, is never given to children as a first name, out of reverence). Guido, a common and respectable male name devoid of any negative con-notations, is the closest name in the Italian language to that of Judas Iscariot, except for Giuda (which, as also mentioned earlier, is also never used as a first name, out of loathing).

By this etymological interpretation, therefore, the two-part Christian-like myth that is *Life Is Beautiful* joins the two stories of Jesus's persecution in the New Testament—the story of his perse-cution as a child by King Herod and of his rescue by his "father" (that is, his mother's earthly companion), and the story of his per-secution as an adult until Judas Iscariot's betrayal and his subse-quent crucifixion by the Romans. Along with the two stories that merge to become a single mythic-theological narrative, the two ar-chetypal Jews—Joseph, the good Jew who saves the messiah, and Judas Iscariot, the bad Jew who betrays the messiah and turns him in to be crucified—also merge here, to become a single Jewish char-acter, Guido.

But this time, in the story's cinematic reincarnation and reinter-pretation, not only does Judas-Guido not betray Jesus-Giosue and cause his death, but he is also the one who saves Jesus. It's because of him that Giosue comes alive out of the shadow of death.

Seemingly, Guido saves Giosue because he's his son. But actually—not only because of his name, but also by the film's plot—in the concentration camp, most notably in the film's final stages, Guido is acting inside Christian myth, playing his part as Judas Iscariot. The film enables this Judas Iscariot to have a radical change of heart and thus achieve rehabilitation.

For, indeed, near the end of *Life Is Beautiful*, three scenes show surprising parallels to the three final events in the life of Jesus Christ—the Last Supper, the betrayal into the hands of his enemies, and the crucifixion. But here they end differently.

Near the film's end, Giosue is suddenly "invited" to a meal—his "last supper." Like Jesus before him, Giosue dines in the company of twelve other guests. (This precise number—"a dozen" in English, "dozzina" in Italian—is explicitly mentioned in Benigni and Cerami's script.) In the New Testament, they are the twelve disciples, who later become, posthumously, the apostles. In *Life Is Beautiful*, they are twelve German children, who don't realize that Giosue is the messiah, the Jew, whom they are actually supposed to hunt down and kill.

Right after the original Last Supper—according to the New Testament, it was the Passover ritual meal that Jesus took with his disciples—Judas Iscariot turns Jesus in to the authorities, who crucify him. But here, in the film, a drastic narrative change occurs. Someone else, a German waiter, informs the authorities about Jesus-Giosue, and Guido-Judas is the one who saves him from capture and death and enables his escape to a new life.

So what happens in this film can be likened to a second coming of Jesus, in which Judas Iscariot is granted by God—that is, by his creator, Roberto Benigni—a chance to redeem himself of his ancient sin, the millennia-old evil he had done by turning Jesus in to his executors. And indeed, he redeems himself in a grand manner by saving Christ and enabling him to come back from the dead.

This interpretation also makes the film's ending coherent. After saving the life of Jesus-Giosue, Guido-Judas sacrifices his own life. As the adult Giosue emphasizes, when looking back on it all: "This is the sacrifice my father made. This was his gift to me."

The role of Guido the Jew in this film can therefore be seen as atonement for the sin his ancestors committed, primarily Judas Is-

cariot, against Jesus, founder of Christianity. And he atones for it in
a grand manner. In the New Testament, Judas hanged himself out of
self-loathing only after it was too late and Jesus was done for. This
time, he sacrifices his own life only after saving the life of Christ.

And if this story is indeed a parable about Guido the Jew, the
reincarnation of Judas Iscariot, saving the Christian boy Giosue,
the reincarnation of Jesus, and giving his own life in return, its
moral can be understood as a religious, theological explanation for
the European Holocaust of the Jews. According to this interpretation, the Jews were punished in the twentieth century for their ancestors' rejecting Jesus and causing his death in ancient times.
Moreover, according to *Life Is Beautiful*, the Holocaust can be seen as
an opportunity the Jews were given in modern times to atone for
their age-old sin.

The Jews, as a Christian article of faith, not only murdered the son
of God who appeared among them, but they also took full responsibility for his murder. And not only upon themselves, but upon all
Jews who would ever be born. As told in the New Testament
(Matthew 27: 15–26):

> Now at that feast the governor was wont to release unto the people a
> prisoner, whom they would. And they had then a notable prisoner,
> called Barabbas. Therefore when they gathered together, Pilate said
> unto them, whom will ye that I release unto you? Barabbas, or Jesus
> which is called Christ? For he knew that for envy they had delivered
> him. . . . But the chief priests and elders persuaded the multitude that
> they should ask Barabbas, and destroy Jesus. The governor answered
> and said unto them, whether of the twain will ye that I release unto
> you? They said, Barabbas. Pilate saith unto them, what shall I do then
> with Jesus which is called Christ? They all say unto him, Let him be
> crucified. And the governor said, Why, what evil hath he done? But
> they cried out the more, saying, Let him be crucified. When Pilate saw
> that he could prevail nothing, but that rather a tumult was made, he
> took water, and washed his hands before the multitude, saying, I am
> innocent of the blood of this just person: see ye to it. Then answered all
> the people, and said, His blood be on us, and on our children. Then re-
> leased he Barabbas unto them: and when he had scourged Jesus, he de-
> livered him to be crucified.[4]

Hence, according to the founding Christianity, all Jews of all generations are guilty of the murder of Christ; the messiah's blood
stains their hands and is engraved on their foreheads like the mark

of Cain for all eternity. And as things are presented in the New Testament, Christianity's primal text, they were the ones who undertook this eternal collective guilt—"on us, and on our children."

And now—as the film seems to present it—almost 2,000 years later, European Jews, the modern offspring of those Jews of antiquity, atone for their ancestors' terrible crime. Millions give their lives in expiation.

Mass extermination? Genocide? Certainly not. What happened in the Holocaust, if anything ever did, was something completely different.

Denying a crime but still justifying it seems to be contradictory, but psychologically the two often go together and complement each other. Often, for example, we hear of a murderer who killed his wife, declaring something like, "First of all, I didn't kill her; and besides, she deserved it, because she cheated on me." This is the same logic used in the argument presented in *Life Is Beautiful*: (1) the Jews were never exterminated, and (2) they deserved it.

The film can be interpreted as justifying the Holocaust because it provides a kind of theological explanation for it, that is, it makes it a "necessary" part of God's cosmic plan. The Holocaust, according to this view of *Life Is Beautiful*, is simply the Jews' deserved punishment, as well as their redemption, for murdering Jesus.

Again I'd like to stress that the film is, as its creator said, a "parable." And in this parable Jesus-Giosue, who survived the extermination camp—that is, came back from the dead—says that the Jew's murder in the camp, just now, is "the sacrifice my father made . . . his gift to me." The moral, then, is clear in its two parts: the nature of the sacrifice, and the nature of the gift.

The moral, first of all, is that the murder of the Jews was nothing but a "sacrifice" that they made themselves, based on their own free will. And a sacrifice, of course, is made to God. That is, the millions of Jews slaughtered in the Holocaust were their own sacrifice to God—as punishment and atonement for rejecting His son, Jesus the messiah, and sending him to be crucified. The Holocaust of the Jews of Europe, according to *Life Is Beautiful*, can be seen as prophetic fulfillment and punishment for Jesus's death, a responsibility that their ancestors willingly took upon themselves and their children, 2,000 years ago.

As for the gift, the second part of the moral says that the Jews' punishment and atonement—that is, their murder—is a great gift that Europe's Jews gave to the Christians. For now, after the Holocaust, Europe can reunite—as the family does in the film, or the parable—as a wholesome Christian family, clean of the taint of Jews. Very possibly, after all these miracles and boons it has received, Europe can even renew its bond with Jesus the messiah and strengthen its faith.

That, if we complete deciphering the moral, is the film's message to the people of European, Western civilization.

And as for the Jews, those who are still alive are generously offered a chance to end to their debt by repaying it: "You killed our messiah, and as punishment we killed—or, to be precise, you sacrificed—so many millions of your number. At last the ancient blood feud between Jews and Christians is settled."

Benigni kills his film's Jew and promptly forgives him his death, even thanks him for his "sacrifice." Does he do it in the name of Christian Europe, which rose to exterminate its Jews and now, some fifty-odd years later, is finally willing to forgive them their extermination?

NOTES

1. Katiuska Bortolozzo, *Il grande libro dei nomi* (Milan: Mariotti Publishing, 1993).

2. *The New Testament*, King James Version.

3. *The Catholic Encyclopedia*, www.newadvent.org.

4. *The New Testament*, King James Version.

Chapter 7

What Is This Film About, Anyway?

The opening scenes of a film almost always hold its entire story and its message in a nutshell. In other words, the film's design and aim are usually evident right from the beginning.

Fellini's *8 1/2*,[1] for example, begins with a scene of a traffic jam, which later turns out to be a dream in which the protagonist (played by Marcello Mastroianni) is stuck. And, indeed, the film as a whole deals with the creative and personal crisis of a film director who feels unable to go on in any direction. *Chinatown*[2] opens with a man looking and groaning with anger at black-and-white photographs taken by the private detective he hired (Jack Nicholson), in which his wife is seen cheating on him. And this is, indeed, a film-noir-style detective thriller, whose plot revolves around a forbidden sexual relationship. *The Silence of the Lambs*[3] begins with an FBI trainee agent (Jodie Foster) running an obstacle course in a foggy wood; one of the trees bears the legend: "Hurt-Pain-Agony—love it." And, indeed, the film later turns out to be about learning and growing up and about owning mental pain and suffering and overcoming them, with the two processes uniting to become an inseparable, single experience.

The opening scenes of these films and of many others clearly foretell the gist of their stories. The same is true for "*Life Is Beautiful*.

The film begins with a voiceover: "This is a simple story but not an easy one to tell. Like a *favola* [fable, fairytale, fiction], there is sorrow, and like a *favola*, it is full of wonder and happiness." The subtitle "Arezzo, Italy, 1939" appears on the screen as the first scene begins.

Under a beautiful, crystalline sky, a Ballila convertible piled high with luggage makes its smooth, happy way through the placid Tuscan hills. FERRUCCIO, a plump young man with a jovial—almost boyish—look about him is driving. His friend, GUIDO, is in the passenger seat. He hugs the wheel as he recites lines of verse in a clear, bucolic tone.

FERRUCCIO: I sing what I see

Nothing gets by me.

(He raises his voice as the car picks up speed, flying downhill.)

FERRUCCIO: "Here I am," said I to chaos, "I am your slave!" "Good!" "For what," said I, "free in the end am I! What good is a caress when bliss . . . this man came to possess?"

". . .Here I am, ready, the trains are gone, the brakes are gone and I can resist no more. . . . Go sweet Bacchus, take me . . . the brakes are gone, oh. . . ." *(In a higher, worried voice.)* The brakes are gone!

(His friend says, from under his hat.)

GUIDO: I heard you!

FERRUCCIO: No, the brakes! They're really gone!

(And he furiously kicks the dead brake pedal. At the first curve the car nearly goes off the road. Guido bounces like a spring and grabs the rolls of upholstery fabric, the car seats, the suitcases.)

GUIDO: Weren't you reciting a poem?

FERRUCCIO: It doesn't work.

GUIDO: Brake! We're going to die! The woods! Brake!

(Guido pulls the hand brake, but it's broken and nothing happens. Meanwhile, the car is gathering speed. It takes a sharp curve, goes off the road, and bounces down into a field, cutting the bushes in its path. Guido falls backward onto the upholstery rolls.)

[In the script, but not in the film, a bump on the ground snaps the trunk open and two rolls of expensive fabric—one white, one gold—unravel and sweep the grass.] *(The car plunges into a tangled grove of thick flowering bramble bushes, ivy, and laurel, and comes out the other side completely covered in branches, leaves, and flowers.)*

(The windshield is covered in twigs and leaves. Poor Ferruccio is now driving blind.)

(Guido stands up, holding on whatever he can, grabbing the windshield and looking ahead, trying to guide his friend.)

The year, we notice, is 1939, when Italy and the whole of Europe are on the eve of the World War II.

So Benigni is depicting here Europe and, by extension, European civilization as a whole on the eve of the most terrible war in history as young and beautiful, rich in culture and technologically advanced, happy and high-spirited, calm and secure, riding forth toward the promising horizon under the clear blue sky. But suddenly, without warning or any detectable cause, an unexpected mishap occurs: European civilization loses its brakes.

The loss of brakes endangers the Europeans as their civilization veers from its course and goes tumbling down a dangerous slope. (Simultaneously, in the script, it loses its religious and moral baggage, as suggested by the white and gold fabric—a distinctly Christian color combination, habitually appearing, for example, in the Pope's mantles and his headdress, as well as in the Vatican's official flag, and traditionally symbolizing the combination of human purity and innocence—white—and the radiance of God's grace—gold.)

Losing its brakes sends the car flying into a dense grove, where it is covered with branches; Europe, therefore, loses the ability to see and to drive, is stricken with temporary blindness, loses its way, and ends up entangled in the thicket.

And where does all this lead?

Here is the film's second scene:

(The King's motorcade is driving on a paved country road, led by motorcycles. Ferruccio and Guido's brakeless car comes out speeding from a side road, inserting itself into the motorcade right after the motorcycles.)
MAN #1: The king is coming.
WOMAN #1: There he is!
GUIDO: It's full of people down there.
(The road straightens and runs through a village where a local festival is in progress, complete with a band and Royalist and Fascist Youth banners and placards. When the crowd of locals, waiting in the shadow of a dais and holding placards that say LONG LIVE THE KING, see Guido and Ferruccio's extravagantly "decorated car" and the motorcycle escort approach, they begin to applaud. . . .)
(Guido, his arm held high and stiff, shouts into the festive pandemonium.)
GUIDO: We have no brakes! Move!
(His gesture is mistaken for the Fascist salute. The villagers raise their arms and shout loud and strong, "Long live the king!")
(The car, festooned with flowers and [in the script] with its train of white and gold fabric, zooms through town and disappears. . . . The crowd of villagers breaks onto the asphalt, saluting the car as it disappears and forcing the royal car . . . in which are seated, in plain sight, His majesty and the queen, to stop short.)

Hence, losing the brakes leads Italy and Europe to Fascism and the Nazi era. (Although in 1939, to be historically accurate, the Nazis were already in power in Germany for six years, and the Fascist regime in Italy was even older; Mussolini seized power in Rome in 1922.)

And where do Fascism and Nazism lead?

This is how the third scene begins:

(The Ballila, free of branches and colorful "drapings," stands dead under the sun in the middle of a dusty dirt road. Guido and Ferruccio are on their backs under the car, trying to repair the damage.)

So—somehow, without showing or explaining how, everything came right in the end; the car has stopped, with nothing happening to it or its passengers.

Already at this early stage, in the opening scenes, the film avoids showing what actually happened to the car, from the loss of its brakes until it came out unscathed—just as later it will avoid showing what really happened during World War II, what happened in the Holocaust, and what Europe did to its Jews.

Furthermore, if indeed the film's beginning represents its plot, then Fascism, Nazism, World War II, and the extermination of millions in the Holocaust—the film's direct subject—are portrayed here as nothing more than a sort of technical glitch or mechanical malfunction. Repair requires merely replacing some loosened screws that fell off with new ones, and Europe will be right back to itself.

And who are those little screws that the magnificent European civilization so carelessly lost during World War II? The film seems to later answer this question: the little negligible screws that Europe lost in the war were the Jews (and presumably the Gypsies and other "undesirables" slaughtered in the camps, although the film doesn't pay them even passing attention). They should just be replaced with some new ones so everything can return to the good old way.

And indeed, just like in the opening scene, the film eventually portrays the mass organized extermination of millions of European people, with the tacit collaboration, at least, of most other Europeans, as a "malfunction," an "unimportant incident," an "amusing episode," a "small screw" that came momentarily loose in the continent's history, culture, and civilization.

The same scene goes on to reveal the film's intention:

(The Ballila, free of branches and colorful "drapings," stands dead under the sun in the middle of a dusty dirt road. Guido and Ferruccio are on their backs under the car, trying to repair the damage. Their voices are heard.)

FERRUCIO *(from under the car)*: Go for a walk. Otherwise we won't get there until tomorrow.
GUIDO: I found the screw. Now what do you need?
FERRUCCIO: Nothing. I need ten minutes alone.
GUIDO: All right, I'll leave you alone. Do you want the screw from before?
FERRUCCIO: No, I want to be alone.
GUIDO: Do I toss the screw if I find it?
(Guido, looking straight ahead as he walks away from the car, notices his black greasy hands.)
GUIDO: I'm going to wash my hands.

Guido's manifest intention cannot, in this context, stand for a mere, innocent, hygienic procedure. The washing of the hands is a powerful metaphor with heavily significant historical, religious, and cultural connotations. Any child raised in European Christian culture will easily recognize it.

The New Testament, as mentioned in chapter 6, relates that the Roman governor Pontius Pilate did everything he could to free Jesus, who came into his custody following Judas Iscariot's betrayal, but Jesus' fellow Jews staunchly refused to receive him, yelling and demanding that he be crucified. Therefore,

> when Pilate saw that he could prevail nothing, but that rather a tumult was made, he took water, and washed his hands before the multitude, saying, I am innocent of the blood of this just person: see ye to it. Then answered all the people, and said, His blood be on us, and on our children. Then released he Barabbas unto them: and when he had scourged Jesus, he delivered him to be crucified.[4]

The script of *Life Is Beautiful* in the original Italian uses an identical expression to the one appearing in the Italian version of the New Testament. The Roman governor's action is described in Italian as "Si lavo le mani" that is—"he washed his hands"—and Guido, in the film, says, "Mi vado a Lavare le mani"—"I'm going to wash my hands."

This expression—"Lavarsi le mani"—has a double meaning in Italian, as its equivalent in Hebrew, in English, and in other languages has. It can mean simply to wash your hands clean or, as in this New Testament scene and in Deuteronomy 21: 6–9, to symbolically "wash away the guilt." When Guido-Benigni says these words at the outset of the film, they can be legitimately interpreted as having either one of these meanings.

These are the words with which Guido, the character created by
Benigni, explains the purpose of the film we are about to see: it seeks
to wash Europe's hands, the hands of Christian civilization, clean of
the Jewish blood it spilled during World War II in the organized, systematic mass extermination later labeled "the Holocaust."

At the end of this final introductory scene, Guido explains not
only what he intends to do in the ensuing film but also how he intends to do it:

> *(Guido gets up from under the car, and looks at his dirty hands.)*
> GUIDO: I'm going to wash my hands.
> *(Close by there's an old farmhouse, surrounded by an orchard and barn. Guido
> walks up to the water pump, fills a pail and washes his hands in the water. He
> notices a young girl milking a cow, and starts a conversation.)*
> GUIDO: Hello, little girl. Where's your mother? How old are you? Is
> she the one who loaded this wagon?
> ELEONORA: No, the landlady did.
> GUIDO: Is it a market? Where's your mother? How old are you?
> What's your name?
> ELEONORA: Eleonora.
> *(Guido bows graciously.)*
> GUIDO: Nice to meet you, I'm Prince Guido!
> ELEONORA: Prince?
> GUIDO: Yes, I'm a prince. All this is mine, this principiant is the prince's
> principiate. We'll name the place Addis Ababa. Out with the cows, in
> with the camels!
> ELEONORA: Camels?
> GUIDO: Even a few hippopotamus! I have to go. I have an appoint-
> ment with the princess.
> ELEONORA: When?
> GUIDO: Now!

Here the introduction ends and the story begins, in the first scene
of the romantic-comedy formula according to which the film is
made, with Dora, who is to become Guido's sweetheart, falling on
him from out of the blue.

But just a moment before—at the end of the introduction, in the
scene quoted above—the film makes clear, through Guido's words,
how it is going to wash Europe's hands of the blood of its Jews: it
will treat the viewers to an ostensibly amusing fake, a sweet fantasy
about the Holocaust that will enable Christian Europe not only to

wash its hands of the guilt but also to lay it squarely on the Jews themselves.

So promises the introduction—and the promise is entirely fulfilled by the ensuing film.

NOTES

1. *Otto e mezzo,* script: Tullio Pinelli, Ennio Flaiano, and Brunello Rondi, director: Federico Fellini, Italy 1963.

2. *Chinatown,* script: Robert Towne, director: Roman Polanski, United States 1974.

3. *The Silence of the Lambs,* script: Ted Tally, based on a novel by Thomas Harris, director: Jonathan Demme, United States 1991.

4. *Il nouvo testamento,* editrice elle di ci, Torino, and allenza biblica universalle (Rome:, 1998).

Afterthoughts: Success Does Not Lie

You can't argue with success, which is precisely why it's very hard to believe that the sensational success of *Life Is Beautiful* is accidental or of no significance. The film resonated profoundly in the hearts of tens of millions of people, so it must have answered some deep emotional need prevalent in the culture.

My argument, which I have tried to justify in this book, is that the great success enjoyed by this particular film, at this particular time, is evidence of a profound, and still growing, need to blot this horrific event out of history, to erase it from the collective memory of Western, Judeo-Christian, European-American civilization, thus enabling this civilization to free itself of the guilt of having committed the Holocaust. After more than half a century, during which the memory and the guilt have stubbornly refused to either sink in or fade away, Western civilization wishes, not for the first time and probably not for the last, to remove the stain. This time, it has attempted to do so with the help of a soothing comic-romantic catharsis, declaring with a seemingly playful wink that it's alright, what's done is done—if it ever was done—but, be it as it may, "life is beautiful" anyway.

The attempt to forget betrays a deep human need. The crime, and the responsibility for it, are indeed unbearable; wishing to be free of them isn't necessarily a sign of moral indifference, perhaps the contrary. If the shame weren't so heavy and disturbing, and the pangs of conscience so piercing, such a tremendous effort to obscure and unmake the guilt wouldn't be made, and the results of this effort wouldn't be met with such a vast enthusiasm.

As an Israeli, as a Jew, I can testify that for us the problem is even more difficult and complex. On one hand, we were the Holocaust's victims—and no one really likes living with a perpetual self-perception of a victim, indeed, the ultimate victim, of what has been often described, not without justification, as "the worst crime in history."

This is not the place to go into a thorough discussion of this venerable question, but by now it's obvious that much of Israeli culture and history, as both have developed in the last fifty odd years, were formed, consciously or not, as a reaction or even an overreaction to the scar left in our psyche by the crime committed against us in the 1930s and 1940s. The Holocaust has become a part of the genetic code of every Israeli, and it seems that of every Jew as well.

On the other hand, even after the Holocaust, we still very much want to be, and do feel like, an inseparable part of that same civilization—Western, European-Christian—that enabled and committed our extermination. Therefore we, Israeli Jews and Jews in general, wish to remove the stain of guilt from Western civilization perhaps as much as the non-Jewish Europeans do, even though some of the latter are direct descendants of those who murdered our parents and grandparents, our people, and our cultural heritage. This stain stings our hearts as deeply, though in a different way, than it does theirs.

And maybe that's the reason for the film's overwhelming, almost hysterical success in Israel as well, the many accolades it received here, and the awards it won—one of which was, ironically, The Mayor of Jerusalem Award for Films about Jewish Subjects in the International Film Festival in Jerusalem.

As someone who wishes to view himself as belonging to Western culture, I wish to pose the question of how we, members of this civilization, choose to deal with the stain of the Holocaust. Do we deal with it like mature, intelligent people, who look the truth in the eye, even though it is unbearable; or would we rather face it—as *Life Is Beautiful* suggests we do—as intentionally deaf and blind, as fools who cannot face the truth and who run away from it by turning it into a sugarcoated, childish lie?

This question is a crucial one for understanding not only the past of our civilization but also its future. If the responsibility for the Holocaust is indeed too heavy to bear, perhaps the only way to make it even a little lighter is to face the past and try to understand its true meaning, to internalize it, to make it an inseparable part of ourselves, and maybe, in this way, make sense of it to a certain extent. The other way—the one offered by *Life Is Beautiful*, which so many of us hurried to embrace—is the way of closing our eyes and sealing our ears, of falsehood, distortion of the truth, repressing it, and avoiding responsibility. Not only does this not make the past easier to bear, but it might also create the circumstances for new catastrophes in the future.

I, for one, refuse to willingly enter Benigni's cute concentration camp, even if its gates, instead of "Arbeit Macht Frei," bear the slogan "Life Is Beautiful." Simplistically reciting that life is beautiful while closing one's eyes will not make it so. Life can and should be beautiful, but it takes a much more serious effort than that.

It's up to us, to our willingness to fight the urge to run away, to hide, and to find comfort in some cute fabrication while our human and moral obligation is exactly the opposite: not to close our eyes, but to look at reality and see it for what it is; not to seal our ears, but to listen carefully and truly hear; and not to conceal the truth behind some foggy cloud, but to try and deal with it, terrible and bitter as it is.

Only then, perhaps, may we be able to learn something.

About the Author

Kobi Niv is head of screenwriting studies at the Department of Film and Television at Tel Aviv University, and teaches scriptwriting at the Department of Communication Studies at Ben-Gurion University of the Negev, and at the Film Department of the School of Arts at Beit Berl College.

Niv is a film critic for a weekly magazine in Israel. Over the years, he has been a satirical columnist for many Israeli newspapers, as well as scriptwriter for the award-winning satirical television program *Nikui Rosh* (*Cleaning the Head*) and for the popular comedy series *Zehu Ze* (*This Is It*).

Together with Israel's top comic artist, Dudu Geva, he has written many popular novels in comic form, both for children and adults. He also wrote the children's play *Hamelech Halach Lishon* (*The King Has Gone to Bed*), which won him the *Kinor David* ("David's Harp") Award for Best Children's Play of the Year, and several books for children, including the critically acclaimed *Abba Sababba* (*The Cool Daddies Store*) and *Haisha Hachi Koeset Baolam* (*The Angriest Woman on Earth*).

He wrote the scripts for the feature films *Shoa Tova* (*Nice Little Holocaust*) and *Eretz Hadasha* (*A New Land*), and three books on scriptwriting and film analysis.